Skopas in Malibu

Skopas in Malibu

The Head of Achilles from Tegea
and Other Sculptures by Skopas
in the J. Paul Getty Museum

Andrew Stewart

THE J. PAUL GETTY MUSEUM   MALIBU, CALIFORNIA

©1982 The J. Paul Getty Museum
17985 Pacific Coast Highway
Malibu, California 90265

ISBN number 0-89236-036-4
Library of Congress catalogue number
82-81304

Library of Congress Cataloging in Publication Data

Stewart, Andrew F.
　Skopas in Malibu.
　　Bibliography: p.
　　1. Scopas, fl. 4th cent. B.C.　2. J. Paul Getty
Museum.　I. J. Paul Getty Museum.　II. Title.
NB104.S7 1982　730'.92'4　82-81304
ISBN 0-89236-036-4　AACR2

Table of Contents

Foreword

Like an apparition from the heavens, a hitherto unknown masterpiece of Greek classic sculpture lights enthusiasm in the heart of everyone who admires it. The name of one of the greatest artists of fourth century B.C. Greece is attached to this marvel. Who would expect to find in a remote French provincial house the over life-size marble head of Achilles, the central figure of the west pediment of the temple of Athena Alea in Peloponnesian Tegea, carved in all probability by Skopas himself? For us, it represents the highest perfection of purely classical Greek art. The master from Paros continued the great tradition of the fifth century and also marked a break with it, introducing a stormy, if not tormented, intonation into its Olympian serenity.

The importance of this monument (acquired in France by Michel de Bry, a well-known Paris collector) was recognized by Professor François Chamoux. The discovery was greeted with approval at the Getty Museum and did not escape the attentive eye of William Wilson, the art critic of the *Los Angeles Times*, who has for years followed the development of our collection of antiquities with understanding and a helpful spirit. He printed a bold article in his newspaper and recommended its acquisition. When the acquisition of the head was unanimously agreed to by the trustees, we had the pleasure of presenting it to the museum visitors and to several specialists, who by good chance were meeting at the Getty.

Few of the antiquities at the museum are of such considerable importance for the history of Greek art as Skopas' Achilles. Our founder would have enjoyed its presence in his museum immensely. Consistent with the policy of the department of antiquities to call on the most competent available specialists for the study and publication of important monuments in our collection, Andrew Stewart, professor at the University of California at Berkeley, was asked to research and publish the piece. Andrew Stewart is indisputably today's authority on Skopas, to whom he has devoted many years of study, including the best extant monograph on the artist. The present publication will help the understanding not only of this new-found masterpiece but also of Skopas' entire oeuvre.

Jiří Frel

Preface:
Skopas Comes to Malibu

In 1977 I first heard a rumor that a "new" head by the great fourth-century Greek sculptor Skopas, of superb quality and in an excellent state of preservation, had appeared on the antiquities market in France. I had published a book on Skopas only a few months before, so I was naturally curious and not a little apprehensive at the appearance of a first-class Greek original supposedly from his very hand—provided, of course, that the piece was an original and not a clever fake, as was rumored in other quarters. I was living in New Zealand and was unable to verify the matter at that time, so I left it aside for the moment.

The next stage in my acquaintance with the head came on a visit to the J. Paul Getty Museum in December, 1978. Dr. Jiří Frel, Curator of Antiquities, asked if I had seen it during its brief exhibit in Paris, and told me what he knew of its history. It was apparently brought to France before 1850, to remain unnoticed in a mansion near Angers until the Parisian collector Michel de Bry acquired it in the late 1960's. It was now on the market once more, and if at all possible Dr. Frel wanted to obtain it for the Getty Museum.

Exactly two months later I received a peremptory telephone call from Dr. Frel: "The head is here, for five days only! Come and see it at once!" By 3 p.m. the next day I was standing in front of the head, which by now had become in my mind an object of almost legendary stature. At once I was sure of two things: it was indeed beautiful, and it had almost certainly come from the pediments of Skopas' great temple of Alea Athena in the southern Greek town of Tegea. As it transpired, my feelings were shared by others. In a lecture delivered in Paris six weeks earlier, Professor François Chamoux had already reached similar conclusions, as had Dr. Frel. After a few minutes, Dr. Frel turned to me and asked, "Well; Skopas?" I said that I thought it was. "Good," he replied, "then if we get it, you shall publish it."

Accordingly, in the acknowledgments that ritually complete an author's preface, I would first like to express my warmest gratitude to Dr. Frel for his generosity in offering me the chance to publish the head and in allowing me full facilities to study and photograph it. His contributions to the thorny problems of its identity and positioning, presented in a seminar at the museum on March 1, 1980 and now published in his preliminary notice in the J. Paul Getty Museum *Journal,* volume 8 (1981), have also been of much value. If we differ, it is only on points of detail.

Next I would like to thank the other participants in the seminar for many helpful suggestions and comments: Mrs. Karl Lehmann, Professor Emeritus of Ancient Art at Smith College and a noted authority on Skopas; Dr. Møgens Gjødesen, Director Emeritus of the Ny Carlsberg Glyptotek in Copenhagen and at that time a visiting scholar at the museum; and M. Michel de Bry, who recognized and later owned the head. If their help is not individually acknowledged at each point, then the fault lies with my memory and Dr. Frel's hospitality—I ask for their indulgence; likewise with my own graduate students, who have helped to sharpen my observations and improve my ideas to no small extent. For help and information on particular points I am indebted to Professors Jean Bony, François Chamoux, and Crawford Greenewalt, and to Mr. Brian Cook; conversations with Dr. Naomi Norman, Professor J. C. Carter, Mr. Bert Smith, and Miss Carlin Barton did much to enlighten me concerning the architecture of the Tegea temple, the Mausoleum friezes, Hellenistic ruler portraiture, and ancient concepts of mimesis, respectively; if I have not wholly subscribed to their ideas in some cases, the responsibility is mine. Professor Loren Partridge, Miss Anne Stewart, and Miss Nancy Tersini deserve my thanks for reading and commenting on the drafts; Mrs. Joanne Heffelfinger, for checking the translation presented in the Appendix; and Dr. Michael Baxandall (although he does not know it), for much of the inspiration that lies behind my approach: *exemplum valde praeclarum ad imitandum.*

For the superb new photographs of the head I must thank Mr. Donald Hull; and for her care in editing this booklet and seeing it through the press, I am indebted to Ms. Sandra Knudsen Morgan. Finally, I must not forget my wife Meriel for her toleration of late homecomings, of several weeks' solo childcare, and of a husband who unaccountably shares his affections with a battered lump of marble.

My two-year love affair with the Getty Museum's head from Tegea has been brief but intense; I hope it will prove to have been fruitful.

Andrew Stewart
Berkeley, California

1. **The head of a warrior (the de Bry Head).** Discovered by chance in a private collection in France, the head of a warrior in Malibu is the finest original marble so far connected with Skopas. It may well be the Achilles from the center of the west pediment of his great temple at Tegea, in central southern Greece. Malibu, The J. Paul Getty Museum. About 350 B.C.

The Man and His Work

Skopas, it is generally acknowledged, was one of the greatest of the Greek sculptors, generally ranked in preeminence with his fourth-century contemporaries Praxiteles and Lysippos. Yet we know nothing at first hand about his life: Cicero, who wrote almost three hundred years after his death, is the first author extant even to mention his name. Indeed, until the appearance of the Getty Museum's head, we were almost as badly informed about his sculpture. Later testimonia to his activity in Greece, the islands, and Asia Minor (see fig. 2) and the identification of workshop pieces and Roman copies—although valuable and occasionally revealing—hardly suffice to fill the void.[1]

The chronology of Skopas' works, as presented to us by these diverse and somewhat heterogeneous secondary sources, falls within the period between 395 and 335 B.C. Actually, most historians now believe that his career proper did not begin until about 380, so that he was probably born a little after 400. He thus lived through a time of great upheaval in Greece, years that saw the collapse of Spartan hegemony, brief resurgences by Athens and Thebes, the encroachments of Philip of Macedon, and finally the crushing of Greek liberty by Philip and his son Alexander at the decisive battle of Chaironeia in 338. We do not know whether Skopas lived to witness Alexander's own great crusade against Persia, which began four years later; but certainly his own work bears eloquent testimony to the turbulence and insecurity that were the hallmarks of his time.

Skopas was a native of the central Aegean island of Paros, distinguished for its quarries of fine white marble and long established as a training ground for sculptors of distinction. With this heritage, his favorite material was naturally marble, both his native Parian and Pentelic from the quarries of Attica; marble is in any case a more supple and receptive medium to the penetrating surface characterization he seems to have sought than is the tense reflectivity of bronze. His favorite subjects were gods and heroes, particularly the younger Olympians and Herakles, and almost from the start of his career he appears as an organizer of large sculptural complexes as adjuncts to architecture. Here, once again, the material was naturally marble. Unlike Lysippos and his following, Skopas apparently made

1

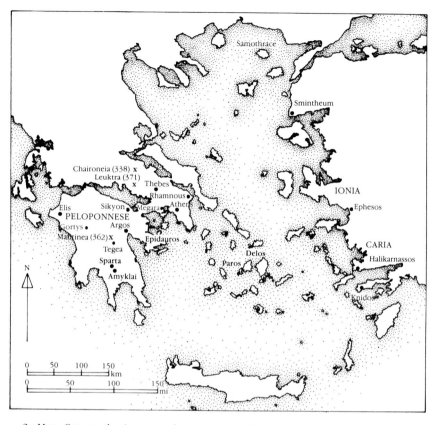

2. Map: Greece, the Aegean and western Asia Minor. This map of fourth-century Greece shows the locations of Skopas' works, as far as they are known to us.

no portraits or athletic sculptures (like the Getty Bronze). As mentioned above, most of his statues have not survived even in copies, and for almost two-thirds of his attested works we cannot even conjecture a date.

Skopas' father seems to have been a certain Aristandros, who worked with the younger Polykleitos on a dedication at Amyklai (near Sparta) to celebrate the decisive defeat of the Athenian fleet by the Spartans in 405.[2] Skopas' own early work also seems to have been done in the Peloponnese. It was apparently quite independent in character: he drew on the traditions of the Peloponnese, Athens, and perhaps eastern Greece too, but did not fall under the spell of any single school or "master" (cf. figs. 3–5). His marble Herakles at Sikyon, of which the Getty Museum exhibits apparently the only complete replica (fig. 6; on loan from the Los Angeles County Museum of Art, formerly in the Hope and Hearst Collections), is clearly early and a somewhat tentative and juvenile exploration of heroic toil and its promised reward.[3] Also early was his bronze Aphrodite Pandemos in Elis, whose image is only preserved today in a few inadequate reflections on coins and reliefs.[4] (The composition, which features the goddess riding a leaping goat, perhaps necessitated this single venture into metal sculpture: marble, with its very low tensile strength, could never have withstood the strain of the cantilevered pose without massive support.) Most importantly, though, he was also commissioned by the Tegeans to build a great new Doric temple for Alea Athena, their guardian goddess (figs. 8, 15–18).[5] All of these projects seem to belong to the years between 380 and 360, although the temple at Tegea certainly took much longer to complete. Its sculptures (the Getty Museum head among them) appear to be later than the middle of the century. The delay was presumably caused by the much reduced and uncertain circumstances of the Tegeans after the collapse of their short-lived Arkadian League in 362 (see Appendix II).

Three works that seem to mark Skopas' early maturity as an artist follow immediately: the Maenad,[6] the Lansdowne Herakles,[7] and an Apollo[8] made for the sanctuary at Rhamnous in Attica. All three appear to belong to the years around 360, and all are known only from Roman copies. The Maenad is preserved in a statuette now in Dresden (fig. 9); the Herakles in the imposing statue from Hadrian's villa at Tivoli, that was one of Mr. Getty's earliest and most treasured acquisitions (fig. 10); and the Apollo in a Roman relief, coin pictures,

3. A warrior. Broken from one of the metopes of the Argive Heraion. This head may stand for the kind of Peloponnesian work from which Skopas apparently drew certain elements of his style, though he rejected the more heavy-handed aspects of its sculptor's handling of facial expression. Athens, National Museum. 420-400 B.C.

4. Head of a Trojan woman. From the east pediment of the temple of Asklepios at Epidauros. With its powerful, cubic structure and fairly compressed features, this head is a direct precursor of Skopas' work at Tegea and elsewhere. Athens, National Museum. About 380 B.C.

5. Two Amazons hunting. Detail from a sarcophagus found in the Royal Necropolis at Sidon. Rather close in style to the Epidauros fragment in fig. 4, these figures (by a Greek sculptor from the Asia Minor coast) also show a distinct similarity to the Malibu head in their sensitivity to skin textures. Istanbul, Archaeological Museum. Early fourth century B.C.

7. **The Genzano herm**. Found near Genzano, Italy. This terminal head, wreathed in white poplar and its hair bound by a heroic fillet, is the best replica of the Herakles type illustrated in fig. 6. The copy was made around 140 A.D. London, British Museum. Original, about 370 B.C.

6. **The "Hope" Herakles**. Formerly in Deepdene House, England. Only rescued from oblivion quite recently, this copy was made by a rather mediocre sculptor in the later second century A.D. It appears to reproduce Skopas' early statue of Herakles awaiting apotheosis, made for the Peloponnesian town of Sikyon: compare the coin in fig. 50. Malibu, The J. Paul Getty Museum, on loan from the Los Angeles County Museum of Art. Original, about 370 B.C.

8. Tegea, site of the temple of Alea Athena. Skopas was the architect of this temple, which replaced an earlier building destroyed by fire in 395 B.C. Apart from the foundations, it was entirely of marble. It fell in an earthquake probably in the fifth or sixth century A.D. Ca. 370–ca. 340 B.C.

and some headless torsos. From the first two it is clear that Skopas, now presumably in his thirties, had succeeded in consolidating his heritage into a strong, supple style of decisive movement and powerful, commanding form, harnessed to a penetrating exploration of human psychology. The Maenad is possessed by powers beyond her comprehension, while the young, superbly fit Herakles appears determined, although perhaps slightly apprehensive, as he faces his future. The Apollo, by contrast, seems to have been generally less mobile and more hieratic in nature, "clad in raiment long, uplifting his voice in song" as the Roman poet Propertius once put it (*Elegies* II. 31.16).

Possibly it was Skopas' realization of his potential as a sculptor of grand and evocative themes, together with his experience in organizing the large workshop needed to build the Tegea temple, that led to his next commission, perhaps the most demanding of his career; the Mausoleum at Halikarnassos.[9] This gigantic project was the brainchild of Mausolos, from 377 to 353 the wealthy ruler of independent and powerful Caria in southwestern Asia Minor.

10. The "Lansdowne" Herakles. From Hadrian's Villa at Tivoli, then in Lansdowne House, London. An imposing statue made in the early second century A.D., the Herakles copies a lost work of Skopas' early maturity (see also fig. 52). It shows the hero after his fight with the Nemean lion (the first Labor), facing the future and all that it holds in store for him. Its head is particularly close to the Malibu head. Malibu, The J. Paul Getty Museum. Original, about 360-350 B.C.

9. Maenad. From Marino (near Rome). This excellent little copy reproduces a statue by Skopas that is vividly described in the ancient sources. The dancer is possessed by the spirit of the god Dionysos and, in her madness, about to tear apart a kid (originally held against her left shoulder). Dresden, Antikensammlung. Original perhaps around 360 B.C.

11. The "Jandolo" head. Once in a private collection in Rome. This head, another replica of the "Lansdowne" type, shows more anxiety in the face than most. This may be either a contribution by the copyist, or a feature of Skopas' original: we cannot tell. Present location unknown. Original, about 360-350 B.C.

7

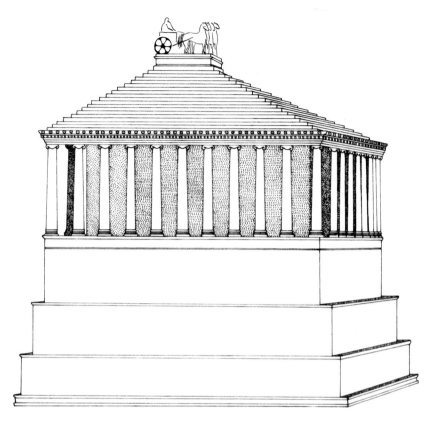

12. **Reconstruction of the Mausoleum, Halikarnassos.** Skopas was employed on this gigantic tomb of the Carian dynast Mausolos, on and off, for about 20 years. Under the architect Pytheos and the sculptor Satyros, he seems to have been responsible, with his colleagues Timotheos, Leochares, and Bryaxis, for the sculptures of the podium. After 367–shortly after 351 B.C.

Construction began in the 360's and was well advanced by Mausolos' death in 353; it finally came to a halt shortly after his wife, Artemisia, died in 351. The building was 140 feet high and measured 120 × 100 feet at its base. Like an enormous rectangular wedding cake, it comprised a massive three-tiered podium topped by an Ionic colonnade and crowned by a pyramid of twenty-four steps, with a huge four-horse chariot at its apex (fig. 12). When finished, it was to contain over three hundred statues—enough for ten temples—ranging in scale from life-size to super-colossal and in subject matter through battle groups, hunting scenes, sacrifices, portraits, friezes

13. **Amazons in battle.** From the Amazon frieze of the podium of the Mausoleum, Halikarnassos. Close in style to the Tegea sculptures and the Maenad, this slab is stark testimony to the brutality of war, as the Amazon in the center is kicked to the ground by a Greek, who then knocks her senseless with his shield as he charges her companion. London, British Museum. About 360 B.C.

14. **Head of the Amazon Melanippe (?).** From the Amazon frieze of the podium of the Mausoleum, Halikarnassos. This head comes from what appears to be the center slab of the east side of the Amazon frieze and could be a product of Skopas' workshop. Though battered, it shows considerable affinities with the Malibu head in style. London, British Museum. About 360 B.C.

of Amazons (figs. 13, 14), Centaurs, and racing chariots, to a menagerie of lions, arranged heraldically around the foot of the pyramid. Skopas himself was allotted the prestigious eastern side of the podium, although his workshop must have done much, if not all, of the actual carving. At any rate, the styles of the few surviving major pieces are very heterogeneous. In addition, the thorough destruction of the building by the Crusaders (it stood, at least in part, until 1421) and the subsequent pillage of the site by Turks and others make any precise assessment of Skopas' own contribution hazardous at best.

Skopas seems to have traveled a good deal when working on the Mausoleum.[10] Presumably after the design stage he was more or less free to do as he pleased as long as he returned every so often to monitor its progress. Statues at nearby Knidos and Ephesos, noted

15. Reconstruction of the temple of Alea Athena, Tegea. Enough survives of the architecture of Skopas' temple at Tegea to permit a fairly thoroughgoing reconstruction on paper. Its severely Doric exterior cloaked an interior that was richly pictorial in character, with Corinthian and Ionic colonnades and a cult triad of Athena flanked by Asklepios and Hygieia. Fabric probably completed around 350-340 B.C.

by the sources but now lost, may belong to this period, as may the great composition of Poseidon, Thetis, Tritons, Nereids on dolphins, and assorted sea monsters.[11] The precise subject of this group is uncertain, but it may have shown either the ferrying of the new armor to Achilles, as described in *Iliad* XIX. 1–18, or Achilles' own journey after his death to the paradise island of Leuke, in the Black Sea. The whole ensemble was apparently taken from Asia to Rome in the second or first century B.C. and is now represented only by a single, somewhat restored Triton in Berlin, and by Roman versions of Tritons and Nereids in Rome, Ostia, and elsewhere.

Skopas may well have visited Tegea during these fifteen years or so of labor for a foreign prince (one is tempted to recall Michelangelo's "enslavement" to the Julius tomb) in order to keep an eye on the great temple, still slowly progressing. At any rate, he was probably back there shortly after 350 to make its cult statues, with at least some members of his workshop. One of them may well have carved the small relief featuring Mausolos' successors Ada and Idreus (351–344) that was found at Tegea early in this century and is now in the British Museum.[12] By this time the fabric of the temple must have been all but complete (fig. 15), and work was getting under way on the sculptures, which to judge by their style seem to postdate the Mausoleum and the Triton. The Roman traveler Pausanias' account of the temple gives some idea of the impressiveness of the project even to one accustomed to the spectacular achievements of the five centuries of Hellenistic and Roman architecture that separated his age from that of the late classic.

> The old sanctuary of Alea Athena was destroyed by a sudden fire...in the second year of the 96th Olympiad [395 B.C.]. ...The present temple far surpasses all other temples in the Peloponnese in size and splendor. The exterior order is Doric, the interior Corinthian; within the temple there is also an Ionic order. The architect, I learned, was Skopas of Paros, who made statues in many parts of ancient Greece, and in Ionia and Caria.
>
> As for the pediments, on the front is the Hunt of the Kalydonian boar. The boar is right in the center, and on one side are Atalante, Meleager, Theseus, Telamon and Peleus, Polydeukes, Iolaos (Herakles' partner in most of his labors), and also the sons of Thestios and brothers of Althaia, Prothoos and Kometes; behind the boar, in addition, are Ankaios, who has already been gored and has dropped his ax, with Epochos supporting him; behind him came Kastor, Amphiaros son of Oikles, and next Hippothoos son of Kerkyon (son of Agamedes, son of Stymphalos); last of all is Peirithoos. On the rear pediment is represented the battle of Telephos with Achilles on the plain of the Kaikos.
>
> The ancient image of Alea Athena, and with it the tusks of the Kalydonian boar, were carried off by the Roman emperor Augustus, after he had defeated Mark Antony and his allies [31 B.C.]. ...It is made wholly of ivory, the work of Endoios. ....The present image at Tegea was brought from the township of Manthyrenses. ...On one side of it stands Asklepios, on the other Hygieia, made of Pentelic marble, works of Skopas the Parian.

Pausanias, *Description of Greece*, VIII. 45.4–47.1 (abridged).

From the rich sculptural decoration of this temple (only part of which is enumerated by Pausanias) about 150 fragments remain, all

16. **Head of the Kalydonian boar.** From the east pediment of the temple of Alea Athena, Tegea. The boar, with its silky coat and wide-open, staring eye, was in the center of the pediment. The virgin huntress Atalante and her lover Meleager were to the left, attacking it with boar-spears (see fold-out plate at end of booklet). Athens, National Museum. Probably 350-340 B.C.

of local marble from nearby Dolianà. This marble was also used for the fabric of the temple. The fragments are divided among the local museum at Tegea, the National Museum in Athens, and now the J. Paul Getty Museum. All the subjects chosen relate to Alea Athena as guardian of the city and its scions, and its hope for years to come.[13]

The cult statues are wholly lost, although an echo of Endoios' archaic Athena has been recognized in a fine bronze statuette from the site, made around 500 B.C. Half a dozen pieces, including two life–size torsos and a head, survive from the nymphs and Nikai that provided the corner akroteria; the central akroterion at each end was a huge openwork acanthus ornament over six feet high. The pediments described by Pausanias are represented by over a hundred pieces, including the heads of the Kalydonian boar and the fallen Telephos (figs. 16, 17). In order to accommodate the boar, the Hunt to the east was carved to a slightly smaller scale than the Kaikos fight to the west, a factor that (as we shall see) is crucial for the attribution of the Malibu head to the latter composition. Finally, thirty fragments

17. Head of Telephos. From the west pediment of the temple of Alea Athena, Tegea. Telephos, craggy-featured and wearing a lion-skin cap to emphasize his descent from Herakles, was the Tegean hero par excellence. To represent his defeat at the hands of Achilles (the Malibu head) in the center of the west pediment was a bold move indeed. (See fold-out plate at end of booklet.) Tegea Museum. Probably 350-340 B.C.

18. Head of a woman. From a metope of the temple of Alea Athena, Tegea. This little head, whose identification remains uncertain, is clearly a workshop piece. The figures of the metopes were not carved in relief but in the round and then doweled on to the slabs of the frieze. Collection Dr. and Mrs. Chris T. Tasulis, Jr. on loan to the J. Paul Getty Museum. Probably 350-340 B.C.

of much smaller scale come from the metopes of the porches, where inscriptions on the slabs indicate that scenes from Tegean legends occupied the east, and the life of Telephos, the west. A small female head in the Getty Museum adds yet another fragment to these (fig. 18), although its precise subject still eludes identification. While the quality of these fragments varies, the style is relatively constant: rugged, compact physiques with rippling, powerful muscles and somewhat cubic heads with craggy jaws, mobile lips, deep-set eyes, and outthrust brows. Expressions are intense, movement is vigorous and energetic, with the figures apparently tightly interlocked within the pedimental space; an action drama par excellence. The promise of the Lansdowne Herakles has now, about a decade later, come to full fruition.

Although many works from this fully mature period of Skopas' career are lost, two that do survive in copies are the Meleager[14] and the Pothos[15] (figs. 19–22). Both attributions, which have sometimes been disputed, are now secured by the head in Malibu. The Meleager, made around 340, presents us with a complex study of the hero of the Kalydonian hunt, seemingly uncertain in his triumph and apprehensive about what will happen when he divides the spoils—an attitude justified by the subsequent quarrels that will soon result in his own death. The Pothos reproduces part of a cult group of Aphrodite and Pothos that stood within the sanctuary of the Great Gods on the northern Aegean island of Samothrace.[16] Here Pothos ("Longing"), who is Desire personified, looks up at the goddess of desire, his whole being expressing a love beyond the capacity of mortals. These statues (the Aphrodite seems lost forever) stood inside a small courtyard whose colonnaded gateway was lavishly adorned with coffer reliefs made, as Professor Lehmann has shown, by Skopas' workshop; possibly the whole building was his work, as at Tegea. At any rate, the complex program of reliefs appears to have featured Philip of Macedon and Alexander. This and other factors combine to date the inception of the work to about 340–338, although like other monuments commissioned by Philip around the time of the battle of Chaironeia it was no doubt still unfinished when he was assassinated in 336.

These projects are the last that can be attributed to Skopas with any confidence. By the mid-330's he was probably about sixty years old, and although we do not know when he died, his career certainly seems to have ended at about this time. Unlike Praxiteles or Lysippos, he left no "school" to continue his work. His approach was too individual and so hardly left room for development in the same ways as did those of his two great contemporaries. He did, however, have a substantial following, as pieces from Athens (fig. 23), Rhodes, and elsewhere amply testify.[17]

By the beginning of the third century, what remained of this individuality had been watered down and submerged into the general current of early Hellenistic eclecticism, so that its specific contribution is limited virtually to the powerful bone structure, deep-set eyes, and "clouded" brow favored, above all, in ruler portraits. His fame, however, did not fade. Revivals of his style took place sporadically during the Hellenistic age, which ranked him with Pheidias and Praxiteles in preeminence.[18]

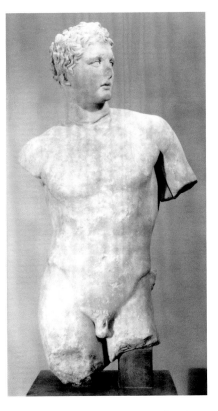

19. **Meleager.** From a Roman villa at Santa Marinella, Italy. This superb replica shows the hero Meleager after the hunt of the Kalydonian boar and before the conflicts over the division of the spoils, which were to lead to his own death. The copyist has adapted the original composition (see fig. 54), placing a staff under Meleager's arm and removing the cloak from his shoulders. Cambridge (Mass.), Fogg Art Museum. Original, about 340 B.C. or shortly thereafter.

20. **Head of Meleager.** Cast of a head found in Italy. One of the best replicas of the Meleager type, this vibrant head is very close indeed to the Malibu head in style, though its slightly more cubic skull suggests a date for the original a little after the Tegea sculptures. Rome, Villa Medici. Original, about 340 B.C. or shortly thereafter.

15

21. **Pothos.** From a villa of the Hadrianic period in Rome. Originally grouped with an Aphrodite, this statue of "longing" is desire personified. The pair, by Skopas, stood in the Sanctuary of the Great Gods at Samothrace. Rome, Conservatori Museum. Original, ca. 340-336 B.C.

22. **Head of Pothos.** From the statue illustrated in fig. 21. This head of the Pothos is the closest of all the known replicas of the type to the Malibu head. It demonstrates in a strikingly clear fashion how Skopas' formula for intense emotion was easily adaptable to markedly diverse subjects and situations. Rome, Conservatori Museum. Original, ca. 340-336 B.C.

23. Head from an Attic gravestone. From Athens. Here, an Athenian sculptor working in the context of funerary art makes use of Skopaic pathos to render the pain of death and parting. Leipzig, Museum der Kunsthandwerk. About 330 B.C.

During the second and first centuries B.C. many of his statues were carried off in triumph to Italy by the Romans, where they were proudly displayed in the squares and temples of the new world capital.[19] There they no doubt served as a continuing inspiration to Roman sculptors, who made copies and versions of them for their aristocratic clients and were happy to appropriate Skopas' more easily imitable mannerisms for their own images of emperors and heroes.[20] Geographers, historians, and connoisseurs went out of their way to list and describe his works, lavishing praise on his achievement. Poets wrote epigrams about his Maenad and included tributes to his skill in their lyrics. Even in the last two centuries of the Empire, when the classical tradition in antiquity was almost exhausted, his contribution to what many still regarded as its golden age could still be recalled with affection, humor, and—on occasion—awe.[21]

24. The Malibu head. This view, from an angle not available to the ancient spectator, shows the unweathered and un-recut side of the head.

18

The Malibu Head
and the Tegea Sculptures

The marble used for the head of a warrior in the Getty Museum probably comes from the Dolianà quarries near Tegea.[1] It is worth noting, though, that its structural homogeneity, fine grain, and predominantly whitish color on the breaks are characteristic of only the best quality stone from these quarries, which can easily be mistaken for good Parian. The more normal output of the quarries— coarser, more heavily tinged with blue, and prone to extensive flaking on the breaks—was used for the majority of the sculptures and for the fabric of the temple. Of the extant fragments of sculpture, only the eastern akroteria employ this unusually high-quality material, fueling the suspicion that the Getty Museum's head indeed held an important place in the ensemble.

The Getty head is so close in dimensions to the remainder of the heads from the west pediment of the Tegea temple that there can be no doubt that it originally belonged to this pediment.[2] For comparison I have included in the notes some measurements from the "brother" of the Malibu head, the helmeted head in the Athens National Museum (NM) 180 (figs. 32, 33, and 35, 36), which also comes from the west pediment. Evidently Skopas must have laid down some canon of proportions in advance, although its principles and method of application (via models, caliper measurements, or written instructions) remain unclear.

The head in the National Museum, like almost all of the other finds from Tegea, is severely battered and has lost its original surface. The head in Malibu, by contrast, is in excellent condition. Its left side is slightly weathered, and a few spots of encrustation remain in the hair and the volute of the visor on this side. There is minor chipping around the flanges of the helmet, on the ears and features of the face, and rather more around the base of the neck. The tip of the nose is missing, as is the left side of the point of the chin. Some of this damage, perhaps caused by a fall from the pediment, was made good in antiquity (see figs. 26–28). Dr. Frel writes as follows.

> A chip on the lower left eyelid was flattened; the drawing of the left volute to the visor on the helmet, the strands of hair emerging under

25. The Malibu head. The powerful structure of the skull is particularly evident in this view.

it, and the helix of the left ear were slightly recut. Both nostrils were retouched and lost a little of their original thickness (the left one slightly more). The most extensive repair was to the upper lip where only the right corner preserves the original surface. The mouth, always open, now shows the upper teeth to their full height (the teeth themselves have been chiseled away and were presumably restored in plaster); the curve of the retouched upper lip is stiff and without elegance, and the lower half of the lower lip lost some of its volume. (Frel 1980, p. 91)

These repairs, competent but somewhat insensitive, were presumably done at the time that the underside of the neck was hacked with a pointed chisel into the form of a convex tenon (fig. 29). A hole for a rectangular dowel, 3.2 cm. square and 3.3 cm. deep, aligned with the front and sides of the neck, was then cut into this in order to secure the join.[3]

Apart from the chiseling needed to effect these secondary repairs, the only other visible tool marks are found on the back of the helmet (left unfinished by the sculptor: fig. 30) where pitting from a coarse punch is overlaid with small dents from a finer version of the same tool, and on the frontlet; whereas on the Athens head a flat chisel was used in long strokes to carve the part between the flanges. The drill was not used at all, it seems, in the original carving: the fine running-drill channel, 2 mm. in width, that now runs across the back of the mouth (fig. 27) is almost certainly secondary, cut at the time that the teeth were recapped. Some signs of abrasion occur in patches

20

26. The Malibu head (detail). The hooded, deep-set eyes and massive orbital bones do much to enhance the intensity of the hero's expression.

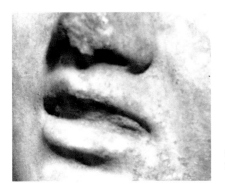

27. The Malibu head (detail). This detail shows the recutting of the lips and teeth by an ancient restorer.

28. The Malibu head (detail). The ancient re-cutting of the lower eyelid is clear in this detail.

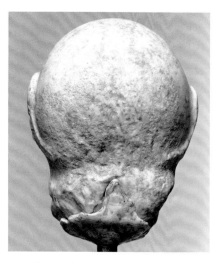

29. **The Malibu head (detail).** When the head was remounted in antiquity, perhaps after a fall from the pediment, the neck was hacked into a rough tenon and a dowel inserted to secure the join.

30. **The Malibu head.** Since the back of the head was masked from view, the sculptor omitted the final finishing of the helmet.

near and around the back of the helmet, although in general it seems that all tool marks were carefully removed before the piece was given a light final polish. The other extant Tegea heads are far less carefully finished.[4] In particular, their sculptors seem to have been prone to use the drill quite often as a labor-saving device, especially in the mouth, nostrils, and ears. Compared with these the carver of the de Bry head stands out as a master of his craft, fit to be ranked with the very best of his predecessors in the fifth century and earlier.

Like his "brother" in Athens, the hero in Malibu wears an Attic helmet with a neck guard (not modeled around the back) and frontlet terminating in volutes, but with no cheek pieces or crest. Since helmets are never worn by the hunters of the Kalydonian boar in mainland Greek art,[5] this helmet, together with the scale of the piece, virtually guarantees that the head belonged, as conjectured, to the west pediment of the temple, whose subject is described by Pausanias as "the battle of Telephos against Achilles on the plain of the Kaikos." (*Description of Greece* VIII. 45.7).

Although the planes of the face are virtually symmetrical, marked distortions occur in the axes of the features, and to a lesser extent

31. The Malibu head. This photograph shows not only how close in style the head of Achilles is to another helmeted head (figs. 32, 33: of Patroklos?) from the temple, but how far superior it is in quality.

32-3. A warrior from Tegea: Patroklos? From the west pediment of the temple of Alea Athena, Tegea. An unrestored cast helps to clarify both similarities and differences between this head, perhaps of Achilles' companion Patroklos, and the Malibu head. Athens, National Museum 180. Probably 350-340 B.C.

34. The Malibu head. Once again, the resemblances — and the differences — between this and the "Patroklos" are clear: compare figs. 35, 36.

35, 36. A warrior from Tegea: Patroklos? From the west pediment of the temple of Alea Athena, Tegea. This view is approximately that of the ancient spectator. "Patroklos...stood beside Achilles / alone, when Telephos turned the valiant Danaoi to flight / and made onslaught on their ships by the sea." (Pindar)

in their modeling. The axes of the eyes and mouth converge to the spectator's left (cf. fig. 31: the distances from the corners of the mouth to the outer corners of the left and right eyes measure 7.9 and 7.5 cm. respectively), and the vertical axis of the face also seems to bow a little to this side above and below. The right eye is longer and narrower than the left, and its eyeball, upper eyelid, and eyebrow and are less strongly curved.[6] These optical corrections follow a pattern that is standard at Tegea and confirm Dr. Frel's observation that the head was designed to be seen as in figures 1, 37, and 46. Evidently it belonged to a figure charging to the spectator's left but turning to look out and up from the pediment.

Although in this position the hero would have stood to a height of 1.70–1.80 meters, only a few centimeters short of the highest point of the pediment (1.90 meters), the top of his helmet was not cut away in order to fit it against the raking cornice, as was the case with the Athens head. The obvious inference, made by almost all of the experts who have seen the piece, is that the hero belonged to the central group of the pediment. If so, who else could the subject be but Achilles, about to deliver the coup de grâce to the fallen Telephos (figs. 17, 45)? One iconographic feature may support this: namely, the prominent locks of hair—unique at Tegea—waving up and over the ears and frontlet of the helmet. These were trimmed away in antiquity on the left side but are still intact on the right. One is tempted to recall Achilles' long golden hair, which he later sheared away to mourn the death of his friend, Patroklos.[7] Archaic and classical vases often show it thus, and within Skopas' own lifetime Alexander was to adopt this hairstyle as his most "Achillean" feature (figs. 58, 62).

Finally, one may point to the superb quality of the head (fig. 37): the carver, if not Skopas himself, must have been his *alter ego*. The head is not only far superior to its fellows from the point of view of sheer technique, but the forms are handled with a sureness of touch unmatched in any fourth-century architectural sculpture that I have seen.

37. **The Malibu head.** Here, too, the camera angle duplicates the ancient spectator's view: "the carver, if not Skopas himself, must have been his alter ego." (p.25)

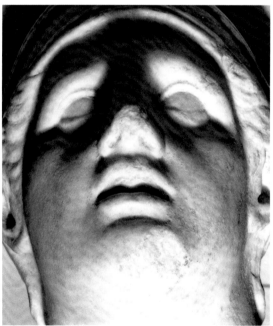

38. **The Malibu head.** This unusual shot is included in order to bring out the increasing complexity of the facial contours: a mounting crescendo of carefully modulated, curvilinear forms.

Looking at the Head

The basic structure is a heavy oval, which because of the flattish cheeks and obtrusive jawbone becomes more angular when viewed from a three-quarter position. Anatomical distinctions are subtle and varied, with powerfully undulating flesh surfaces. These overlie a skull that is solid and massive yet neither particularly obtrusive (except at certain key points, such as the ridge of the nose or the point of the chin) nor unduly schematic, as in the other heads. To this end, figure 38 gives some idea not only of the sheer plastic strength of the piece but also of the subtlety with which the morphology of the major structural features is handled. Thus the carefully modulated, increasingly complex contours of chin, lips, nostrils, cheeks, and brow form a mounting crescendo of projecting shapes as the eye travels up the face—an effect that is particularly well tuned to the angle of the head and its intended position in the pediment from the perspective of the spectator on the ground below.

One may also note that the sculptor never uses sharp cuts or ridges to mark transitions between planes, a mannerism found time and again at Tegea, particularly at the junction of the chin and neck, in the naso-labial furrow, around the orbital portion of the upper eyelid, and above the bulge of the forehead (the so-called "clouded brow" or—in the Renaissance—"Michelangelo bar").[1] Instead, muscles interlock tightly but without noticeable discontinuity, rising and falling according to the dictates of the bone structure that underlies them and the movement that animates them. This surface animation is itself complementary to both the bone structure and the muscular activity generated by the movement and the facial expression, not independent of them as in so much Hellenistic sculpture. The yielding textures and vigorous, complex modeling around the lips, nostrils, and eyes shade by almost imperceptible degrees into the tauter, harder, and more ample planes of the chin, cheeks, nose, and forehead, which in turn balance and contain the emotional intensity of the expression.

Yet despite its penchant for rounded, undulant surfaces and thick but subtly differentiated skin textures, the style seems to be purely glyptic, as one would expect—a marble carver's style with no real hint of the more additive, unstable character that would betray an

39, 40. Head of Perseus (?). From a statue found in a Roman wreck off Antikythera, in southern Greece. A late work of the Polykleitan school, this piece shows a marked conservatism when compared with the self-assertive style of the de Bry head. Athens, National Museum. About 350 B.C.

origin in the freely modeled forms of wax or clay, as cast into bronze.[2] It is perfectly possible, however, that among other factors the increasing interest in the kind of surface richness displayed in the Getty head could have led later artists to adopt modeling techniques and their associated formal characteristics in free-standing sculpture, first bronze and then marble. In this sense alone the de Bry head stands on the brink of the Hellenistic age.

The basic principles of Skopas' style, as filtered through the hands of his apprentices and employees at Tegea and elsewhere, have been clear in outline for almost a century. The Getty Museum's head now enables us for the first time to compare his achievement directly with the work of the two major contemporary schools of sculpture, the Polykleitan and the Attic (figs. 39, 40 and 42, 43). The two statues of heroes illustrated here show how broad the differences had become between Skopas and his contemporaries, even those to some extent (as here) under his influence, by the 340's and 330's.

The bronze "Perseus" from Antikythera (figs. 39, 40) seems to have been made by a late follower of the great Peloponnesian artist Polykleitos (active ca. 460–410 B.C.).[3] Polykleitos worked almost

41. **The Malibu head.** The thrusting vibrancy of the Skopaic hero contrasts markedly with the reserved poise of the Polykleitan.

exclusively in bronze, and specialized in statues of heroes and athletes that were both meticulously planned (according to a mathematical canon of proportions) and finished with a care that was evidently almost obsessive. He had numerous followers, and the "Perseus" is a work of this school in its last stages around the middle of the fourth century, when the new, dynamic style of Lysippos was increasingly luring bronze workers away from the older, more conservative modes of rendering the human form.

In the head of this statue something of the large skull, flatter cheeks, and massive jaw of the Malibu head are clearly visible, but the dominant structure is still a broad Polykleitan oval, with little of the angularity and compression of the features of the Malibu head or of its deep, heavy chin and craggy, high-arching brow. In profile the chin, cheeks, and forehead lie almost on the same perpendicular, whereas on the Skopaic head in Malibu the central part of the face and the nose push forward to form a convex, powerfully dynamic silhouette. The flesh, too, is modeled in an understated and economical way, with not a hint of the exuberant surface richness and broad, dynamic muscularity of the Malibu head.

The features, despite a certain degree of intensity often ascribed to Skopaic influence, are small and precise and accentuated by the sharp transitions that demarcate them clearly from the chin, cheeks, and forehead. The mouth, slightly open and turned down a little at

42, 43. The "Aberdeen" head. From Greece. A masterpiece in the style of Praxiteles, this head of a young hero (Herakles?) is modeled with fastidious attention to delicate nuances of light and shade. London, British Museum. About 330 B.C.

the corners, is serious but not grim; the nose is rather narrower and rounded along its ridge, and the nostrils are neat; the eyes are neither hooded nor particularly deep-set.

One's over-all impression is of a costive style, desperately anxious to remain true to its principles of balance, moderation, and abstract harmony of form while cautiously attempting to bring itself up to date. This is exactly what one would expect from a century-old tradition near the point of exhaustion. Clearly, whatever Skopas may or may not have learned from Peloponnesian sculpture in his youth (cf. figs. 3, 4), by his maturity he had little in common with it apart from an equal dedication to strongly muscled, assertively athletic physiques. Indeed, in the realm of facial structure and expression he had now become the donor and no more the recipient.

As for the Aberdeen head (figs. 42, 43), the close relationship between this and the Hermes of Praxiteles (whether the Hermes is itself a copy or an original is mercifully irrelevant to our present concerns) establishes it as distinctively Attic.[4] Unlike Polykleitos, Praxiteles (active ca. 375–330 B.C.) worked mostly in marble and specialized in statues of gods and demigods, modeled with a tender softness fitting to the inhabitants of a dreamy paradise far from the

44. **The Malibu head.** "Common to Skopas and Praxiteles are only the externals of their styles: a shared appreciation of the expressive potential of deep-set eyes, mobile lips, richly characterized musculature, and an equally close attention to the matter of skin-texture." (p. 32).

cares of men. The Aberdeen head, if not carved by him in person, is certainly in his manner although it is rather more robust in execution than the Hermes; its subject was probably a hero, possibly Herakles. Like the Getty Museum head, it is of higher quality than any photograph can convey.

In the Aberdeen head, the oval of the face is rather longer, the structure more finely differentiated than either the "Perseus," which is almost schematic, or the de Bry head. The brow is equally wide, although differently shaped, and the cheeks are nearly as long. Yet the chin is far smaller—almost, considering the subject, petite—with a pronounced dimple at its point. The bone structure is altogether less obtrusive; for instance, the ridge of the nose, although broad, is gently rounded and fleshy, as against the hard, flat, fascia of the Malibu head's nose. The forehead sags somewhat in the center and the mouth is set relatively low, as if the sculptor has wished, by so drawing out the features of the face, to endow it with a slightly moody character. In profile, the facial angle sheers away so that the forehead markedly overhangs the nose, cheeks, and lower jaw, and the chin recedes still further. Against the jutting nose and aggressively massive jaw of the Malibu head, or even the measured and carefully balanced profile of the "Perseus," the effect is of a more sensitive and introspective personality than the vehement Skopaic hero or the somewhat bland Polykleitan.

The sculptor's handling of detail strengthens this impression: the modeling is vibrant and soft, especially about the features where tender pads of flesh and delicately handled transitions surround the full, sensuous lips and rather small, carefully hooded eyes. Compared with the short-clipped, caplike mop of hair of the "Perseus" or the softly undulating waves of the de Bry head, the hair of the Aberdeen head is treated as a thick, tousled mass deeply penetrated by irregular furrows and cavities. This, together with the handling of the flesh surfaces, gives the impression of a conscious exercise in chiaroscuro, a deliberate address to the expressive potential of carefully modulated light and shade.

Here, then, one recognizes a style that is finely tuned to the most delicate nuances of mood, whose every component is gauged for optical effect rather than envisioned as a descriptive rendering of formal detail. Compared with such minutely calculated impressionism, the powerful, thrusting plasticity and straightforward (if somewhat indeterminate) pathos of the Malibu head are indeed a world away. Common to the two sculptors are in fact only the externals of their styles: a shared appreciation of the expressive potential of deep-set eyes, mobile lips, and richly characterized musculature, and an equally close attention to the matter of skin texture.

This last remark perhaps requires some amplification, if only because it seems that differentiation of such textures was a matter of consuming interest to fourth-century sculptors. The surface modeling of the Aberdeen head is closely predicated on the bone, muscle, or fat below it, and its subtle modulations of surface are responsive to every modification in the character of the underlying tissue. On the Malibu head, however, the envelope of flesh is perceived to be an entity in its own right, firmly encasing yet distinct from what lies below. This style of modeling—smooth, dense, fairly homogeneous, and somewhat opaque—may owe something to East Greek work of the early part of the century and before (cf. fig. 5), although the solidity and clarity of the structure immediately dissociate the piece (and the rest of the Tegea sculptures) from any presumed affiliation to a supposedly still vital Ionian school of carving.[5]

This matter of skin textures is difficult to discuss not only because photographs hardly do justice to it, but also because the English language is not particularly well endowed with a working vocabulary to describe it. Yet to the Greeks of the fourth century the description and analysis of such textures were issues of no little concern, as their extant writings demonstrate. These writings, in turn, are but a part of a larger whole, the science of physiognomics, whose earliest supposed practitioners, Hippokrates and one Zopyros, worked in the mid-to-late fifth century. Their writings on the subject do not survive, however, and neither do those of their immediate followers; so it is not until Aristotle's *Analytica Priora* of about 340 that we can make any definitive contact with the subject (II. 27, 70b7–39). Scattered references also occur in other works of his, and then follows a complete treatise, the *Physiognomonica,* compiled around 300 B.C. from an abridgment of the writings of his pupils, the Peripatetics.[6]

Unfortunately, although this book devotes much space to the question of skin textures (see Appendix I), it is a distinctly jejune and slippery document. Its tone is sophomoric, and the complex terminology it uses with such abandon is rarely defined. Add to this the fact that the sculpture itself is hardly less difficult to pin down, at least on this level, and the prognosis is hardly encouraging. Sadly, it seems that for the present, text and image must remain apart, while on his side the observer must stay alert to the existence of a dimension of ancient experience that may always elude him.

If this discussion has achieved nothing else, it should have shown on the one hand how refined the Tegea style could become at the hands of a master, and on the other—by comparison with the "brother" of the Getty Museum head, Athens (NM) 180—how easily it could be simplified into a workshop style, a formula capable of rapid assimilation by journeymen–carvers and suitable for mass production in the context of the large ensembles that were Skopas' speciality. At Tegea in particular, this requirement was apparently urgent:[7] the building contract for the temple, the preamble of which is preserved intact (Appendix II), shows a most unusual preoccupation with possible interruption of the work by labor troubles and enemy action. As to the first of these possible impediments we have no further information, but the threat of war was no trifle in view of the bitter power struggles of these years. The seven more or less complete heads from the pediments and akroteria (about 15 percent of the original total) are all by different hands; this and the rather cursory (but by no means incompetent) execution of many of the surviving fragments suggest a large workshop in a hurry. Here once again, if not in some other respects, Skopas the driving entrepreneur and Praxiteles the fastidious loner seem to stand at opposite poles of fourth-century sculptural practice.[8]

45. Telephos. From the west pediment of the temple of Alea Athena, Tegea. Trapped in Dionysos' vine at the very moment of victory, the hero looks up helplessly toward his attacker, Achilles. Tegea Museum. Probably 350-340 B.C.

46. The Malibu head. Achilles towers over the fallen Telephos, but at the crucial moment his attention is distracted — by Athena, come to save her protégé?

47. Greeks versus Amazons. From the Amazon frieze of the podium of the Mausoleum, Halikarnasssos. This slab gives, in mirror image, an idea of what the center of Skopas' pediment may have looked like. Telephos, though, was more stoical than the fallen Amazon at center, who screams in terror to her companion to save her. London, British Museum. About 360 B.C.

34

The Center of
the West Pediment

If the head of a warrior in the Getty Museum could indeed be the
lost Achilles from the western pediment of Skopas' temple, this
naturally has important consequences for the composition, iconography, and interpretation of the central group as well as for the
scene in general. As Pausanias tells us, somewhat laconically, the
pediment featured "the battle of Telephos with Achilles on the plain
of the Kaikos."[1] The background of this episode is as follows. Auge,
daughter of king Aleos of Tegea and priestess of Alea Athena, was
seduced in the sanctuary of the goddess and made pregnant by
Herakles. At this violation of her sacred temenos the virgin goddess
cast a blight over the country. When her son was born, Auge hid
him in the precinct but was discovered by Aleos when an oracle
revealed to him the cause of the blight. He then promptly sealed his
daughter in a box and cast her out to sea, leaving her baby, Telephos,
to die on nearby Mount Parthenion.

Fortunately a hind found the child and suckled him, and even more
luckily Herakles appeared and gave him to shepherds to raise. When
he reached manhood, wanting to know the identity of his real
parents, Telephos consulted the oracle at Delphi. He was told that
he would find his mother in Mysia (near Troy), whither her box had
drifted "by Athena's foresight." She was now married to Teuthras,
the king of that land. Teuthras welcomed his stepson, married him
to Hiera, his own daughter by a previous wife, and named him his
successor.

Shortly afterwards the Greek army landed in Mysia on its way to
Troy and, mistaking it for Troy itself, began to plunder the coun-
tryside. Telephos, now king, met them in battle by the river Kaikos
and put the army to flight. But (unlike the Greeks) he had failed to
make a sacrifice to Dionysos before the encounter. The angry god
caused Telephos' foot to become entangled in a vine miraculously
conjured up in the hero's path. He duly tripped and was speared in
the thigh by Achilles, who with Patroklos was covering the Greek
withdrawal. After wreaking further havoc, including killing Hiera,
the Greeks sailed away. The wound refused to heal, and yet another

oracle at Delphi revealed that it could only be cured by whoever had inflicted it. Telephos then disguised himself as a beggar and went to Argos, whither the Greeks had been driven by a storm. Gaining admission to the palace, he revealed himself to Queen Klytemnestra. She was thirsting to revenge the death of her daughter Iphigeneia at Agamemnon's hand (supposedly to appease the gods and allow the fleet to sail for Troy once more). At her suggestion, Telephos seized Agamemnon's infant son, took refuge on an altar, and compelled the king to make Achilles cure his wound. Achilles did this by applying rust from the lance that had caused it. The two sides became reconciled and Telephos agreed to guide the Greeks to Troy.

With this story in mind, and regarding the pediment from the spectator's viewpoint (see the fold-out plate at the end of this booklet), one must presumably imagine Telephos (fig. 45) to be down on one knee to left of center. He is trapped in the roots of the vine maliciously conjured up by Dionysos, and his left thigh is transfixed by Achilles' spear. He looks up to our right toward the adversary who towers over him (fig. 46) yet whose advance has momentarily come to a halt, for some inexplicable reason.

Since the bodies of both combatants were angled toward the spectator's left, it is evident that for the composition to regain its balance, a third figure must have been inserted to left of center, presumably protecting the fallen Telephos by counter-attacking towards Achilles. The arrangement on the west pediment would then echo that on the east, where Atalante and another hero lunged from left and right of center, respectively, over the wounded body of the boar. Such triads are extremely common in fourth-century architectural sculpture. Among numerous examples from the Amazon frieze of the Mausoleum, one may cite (in mirror image) British Museum 1009 (fig. 47) where an Amazon tries to protect her fallen comrade from a charging Greek, who glances out toward the spectator in a way very similar to the de Bry warrior.

The identity of this hypothetical third figure is uncertain, but one obvious candidate is Hiera, Telephos' wife.[2] On the (admittedly insubstantial) evidence of Philostratos, who around A.D. 200 wrote our only full-length account of the battle, she was killed by Nireus shortly after Telephos was wounded. He describes her, however, as mounted at the head of a troop of Amazon-like Mysian women, who would hardly have fitted into Skopas' pediment—although they were included in the Telephos frieze of the Great Altar of Pergamon some two centuries later. Philostratos attributes Telephos' rescue to the intervention of unnamed "Mysian warriors," but as with Hiera, no fragments exist at Tegea to settle the matter one way or the other.

If this reconstruction is anywhere near correct (and the positions of the two main figures, Telephos and Achilles, are hardly in doubt), quite striking similarities begin to emerge in both composition and narrative structure between the two pediments. In both cases the victors were advancing from the spectator's left, as is normal in Greek art, while heroes who had previously received the worst of things rallied for a counterstroke to the right. Thus, in the left half of the east pediment, as we know from Pausanias and the remains themselves, Atalante and Meleager delivered the coup de grâce to the boar; and on the right, although Ankaios had been gored and his companions thrown into confusion, several fragments suggest that two or three of the hunters had managed to gather their wits enough to attack the beast from behind.[3] As for the west pediment, we know that Telephos was brought down in the moment of victory, so one must imagine his victorious Mysians also moving from left to right, attacking the retreating Greeks as they went. Achilles and Patroklos were the only ones to withstand the onslaught, according to Pindar in his ninth *Olympian Ode*:

> [Patroklos] went with the Atreidai
> To the plain of Teuthras, and stood beside Achilles
> *Alone*, when Telephos turned the valiant Danaoi to flight
> And made onslaught on their ships by the sea.
>
> (IX. 70–73)

So if the Malibu head is indeed Achilles, then it seems reasonable to suggest that the Athens head could be his surrogate, Patroklos (figs. 35, 36).[4] Clearly this figure was also moving "against the tide" and, judging by the posture, as evidenced by the musculature of the neck and the cutting across the crown of the helmet to fit it against the top of the pediment, it cannot have stood more than a meter or two from the center.

Although many matters of detail clearly remain open, their eventual resolution cannot seriously affect the primary problem posed by the de Bry head. What has distracted Achilles, and why is he looking open-mouthed out of the pediment and up to the sky? In formulating an answer, one must be aware that the slightly mawkish expression of the mouth is due to the ancient restorer, not to Skopas. The recutting of the lips has left them rather flat and lifeless (fig. 26: compare the Athens head here), and in particular the removal of the teeth (presumably replaced in plaster) has hardly served to improve the hero's temper. I suspect that the original expression probably had more of a snarl in it than his present rather vacant gasp of surprise.[5] Only this slightly more open mouth distinguishes Achilles' facial expression from that of his victim, Telephos (fig. 45). The Skopaic formula is decidedly uniform, whether applied in the context of fear, surprise, hate, or (as fig. 22 testifies) love—and is also remarkably flexible. The emotion it conveys is a generalized one until differentiated by bodily behavior, and so in itself is somewhat indeterminate.

One may suggest two possible sources of distraction: Achilles is looking up either at the Nikai akroteria that stood above the corners of the pediment, or at Athena, who has appeared in the sky, unseen by all but him, to command him to spare the hapless Telephos.[6] After formerly inclining to the first theory, I now tend to favor the second, originally proposed by Dr. Frel, for several reasons. First, the Malibu warrior clearly does not look toward either corner of the pediment (contrast here figs. 35, 36): rather, he looks up and out, almost along the central axis of the temple. Second, the placing of Telephos to the left of center—the victor's side—has long been recognized as significant: contrast here the more conventional format of BM 1009 (fig. 47). This may be construed, therefore, as the side of *ultimate* victory, and indeed Telephos' fall came in the moment of triumph when he had successfully routed the Greeks. Not even properly defeated but only checked from his rightful victory, it is he, if anyone, who should be receiving comfort from the Nikai at the corners.[7]

As for Athena, although no text testifies to her direct intervention, this omission is hardly decisive since only one really comprehensive account of the fight survives and that is late and rhetorical, the *Heroicus* of Philostratos. Indeed, some scholars, recognizing the need for some device to rescue Telephos from his plight, have sought in the past to restore Athena as a counter to Dionysos in the pediment itself.[8] Yet the vine would have rendered the presence of Dionysos somewhat otiose; no physical evidence for either deity exists among the preserved fragments, and, with the discovery of the de Bry head, it is almost impossible to conceive how such an arrangement would have worked. Still, the argument that only a deus ex machina could really have sufficed to stem the onslaught of Achilles is a strong one. As the protectress of Telephos throughout his wanderings, and as the titular deity of the temple, Athena is the obvious candidate. The impact of her sudden intervention from above, unseen by any except Achilles, would in such circumstances have been stunning indeed: a dramatic reversal or *peripéteia* of an intensity almost worthy of the great fifth-century tragic poet and author of several plays on both the Telephos and the Meleager legends, Euripides.[9]

Tegea suffered much at Spartan hands between the collapse of the Arkadian League in 362 and the Macedonian-imposed settlement of the Peloponnese after the battle of Chaironeia in 338.[10] Given such setbacks, together with the direct evidence of the building contract (see Appendix II), one may legitimately wonder whether reference to the tribulations of the times, not to mention hope for divine aid in banishing them, might not have been deliberately intended by the managing committee of *esdotéres* or whomever else directed the choice of themes. One may contrast the marked avoidance of such a strong narrative accent on what seems to be the central slab of the east frieze of the Mausoleum, BM 1007-8-10, reportedly also by Skopas (fig. 14).[11] Clearly, to portray the crisis point in the career of a national hero on the premier temple of his native city was a far cry from providing four hundred feet of appropriate decoration to crown the podium of a barbarian prince's tomb.

48. Priam. From the east pediment of the temple of Asklepios, Epidauros. Priam, his face contorted, screams in agony as Neoptolemos grasps his hair and stabs him in the side. Skopas, it seems, reacted strongly against extreme pathos of this kind. Athens, National Museum. About 380 B.C.

The Wrath of Achilles

Although it is evident that in many ways the Getty Museum's head raises more questions than it answers, a synthesis of some kind seems due at this point. The head can then be placed in its wider context, namely, the late classic style of the fourth century B.C. At Tegea, Skopas deliberately pursues economy, lucidity, and clarity of presentation. To these ends, he regularizes the facial expressions of his heroes within the constraints of a single, powerful formula, suitable for both victor and vanquished alike (figs. 45, 46). In this way, he achieves something of an accommodation with the dictates of classic taste and the absolute values of an earlier age. He thereby stabilizes, fixes, and ultimately projects the sheer heroic prowess of his characters directly into the startled observer's consciousness.

As one would expect, the Greeks had a word for such prowess, for one's "strength relative to one's world." That word was *areté*—in a heroic ambience such as this, a combination of divine favor, high birth, inner fortitude, and of course absolutely unmatched muscle-power.[1] By the very force of Skopas' rendering one is compelled to admit that these men—Telephos and Achilles—are possessed of towering *areté*. They are titanic individuals, constant in their values (a constancy mirrored in their firm-set features), close knit as a class (for physically and emotionally there is little to choose between them), undeviating in their dedication to the heroic enterprise, and mighty in their strength relative to the world.

A brief comparison between Telephos and the Priam from the east pediment of the temple of Asklepios at Epidauros, carved about 380, will serve to exemplify Skopas' achievement in the generation that separates the two works (figs. 45, 48).[2] Both kings are caught in a similar trap, but to the iron resolution and indomitable will of the Telephos, contrast the weakness, vacillation, and total capitulation to his emotions of the Priam. The heroic world now co-opts those emotions that on the Argive Heraion (fig. 3)[3] and at Epidauros had begun to threaten its destruction—for, all else apart, an emotion-tossed and inconstant hero risks being no hero at all, as Euripides well recognized and often used to his advantage. In the process, it purifies and welds them into a single, all-embracing expression of battle fury appropriate to the war-fixated nature of a true hero's character.

41

The classical Greek term for such an emotion was, quite simply, "Ares,"[4] while its epic equivalent was *lússa*[5] (personified as divine force by the later fifth century). Its effects are most vividly described in the *Iliad*. Here Achilles' *lússa* after his battle with Skamander "ever gripped his heart, in his craving to win him glory" (XXI. 542–43), while Hektor's *lússa* is said to drive him onward "like a burning flame," so to possess him that "exulting greatly in his might, he raged furiously, trusting in Zeus and heedless of men or gods" (IX. 237–39; XIII. 53). As in Skopas' work, in Homer an emotion of this kind vents itself through the mouth, the nostrils, and above all the eyes, where fire metaphors are particularly appropriate. Thus when Achilles arms for battle, "a clash went from the grinding of his teeth, and his eyes blazed like a flame of fire" (XIX. 365–66), and Hektor pursues the Greeks into their camp "with the eyes of the Gorgon, or of Ares, bane of men" (VIII. 349). By the time of Aristophanes, the snarl of rage is a commonplace in literature, and one can even "look Ares" (*Peace* 620), a phrase that ought to have been in Skopas' mind as he worked on these pediments.

The power of a hero's facial features to project his character into the world may serve to reintroduce one final contributor to Skopas' complex of metaphors for fixity of purpose and truly heroic *areté*. This is the science of physiognomics, whose history was briefly discussed on pp. 32-33.

In the physiognomic literature the technique employed is relatively simple: men's characters are judged from their physical appearance, by collecting and comparing recognizable physical characteristics or "signs" that are seen to be associated with certain kinds of animal behavior. In animals, character types tend to correlate with species in a fairly straightforward manner: thus monkeys are dull, cattle lazy, dogs sensitive, and so on. Their individual "signs" (small heads, dry skin, lank hair, or whatever) may be paralleled in man, and human character read from them. Strange as this procedure may seem to us, its influence has been extraordinarily pervasive and longlived: the last major treatise in the field was enthusiastically supported by none other than Goethe.[6]

When I studied the Tegea sculptures some years ago, I found myself at a loss to account for the radical break with tradition that they undoubtedly represent. The combination of massive, often almost cubic skulls, thick noses, deep-set eyes, bulging brows, rather bristly hair, craggy muscles, and energetic movement is unprecedented in

Greek sculpture. The *Physiognomica* seems to supply the answer at once, in its description of the lion, who personifies the male type in its most perfect form.[7]

Its mouth is good-sized, its face rather cubic and not too bony; the upper jaw does not overhang but equally balances the lower, the nose is quite thick, the eyes bright and deep-set, neither very round nor very narrow, but of moderate size. The eyebrow is large, the forehead rectangular, rather hollowed in the center but overhanging toward the brows and again toward the nose like a cloud. Above the forehead towards the nose, the hair parts to the sides and tends to bristle; the head is of moderate size and the neck long and correspondingly thick, covered with tawny hair, neither too bristling nor too curly at the ends. About the collarbone the lion is loose rather than close-knit; his shoulders are strong; his chest is powerful; his frame is well formed with large ribs and back, lean haunches and thighs, and strong, muscular legs. Indeed, his whole body is well joined and muscular, neither very hard nor very moist. He moves slowly with a long stride and swings his shoulders as he goes. These then are his bodily characteristics: in character he is generous and liberal, noble and a lover of victory, yet gentle, just and affectionate toward his associates.

Physiognomica 5. 809b14–26

In Greek literature, to compare heroes with lions is as old as Homer, and on archaic black-figure vases fights over the fallen are often aptly accompanied by predella pictures showing two lions battling over a bull or a deer.[8] Skopas, one could argue, simply went one step further and translated the findings of contemporary physiognomical science into art—an unprecedented conceptual leap, if true. Herein lies an explanation of the artistic roots of his mode of presenting the hero: although some of its elements are recognizable, in embryonic form, on the Argive Heraion (fig. 3), at Epidauros (fig. 4), and elsewhere (fig. 5), the whole so far transcends the parts that to all intents and purposes it is tempting to class it as an invention from scratch. In fact, its true roots seem to lie in somewhat different soil, in Skopas' almost atavistic dedication to the ancient concept of the lion–man, as refined and redefined by contemporary physiognomers.[9]

In the world of Skopas, as formerly in that of Homeric epic, individual men of might, "lion-hearted heroes," may once again carve out their destinies with considerable autonomy; yet, as there, the gods must never be forgotten. On both of the Tegean pediments, divine pique or *phthónos* is the immediate cause of the trouble; in the east on the part of Artemis, in the west on the part of Dionysos.[10] As Phoenix explains in his lengthy discourse on heroic *areté* in *Iliad* IX, just as the gods' *areté* and strength are greater than the *areté* and strength of their human counterparts, so too are the gods more touchy about them. It is certainly no coincidence that Phoenix then launches into a full-scale account of the Kalydonian hunt and its aftermath of feuding and murder, with great stress on the causative role of Artemis and her *phthónos*.

At Tegea then, as in Homer, one comes to realize that the gods, often unseen, are to be recognized as manipulators, their motives frequently opaque, their wrath terrible in its consequences, and their affections often dangerous even to their protegés. As Menander was pithily to remark a few years later, "he whom the gods love dies young" (fr. 125 Kock). For proof of this last statement one has only to remember Achilles. So if he is to be true to his calling, the real hero (victor or vanquished) simply has no choice but to do and to endure. Alea Athena cannot avert the course of Fate. She can only (with Asklepios and Hygieia) seek to mitigate its effects or help to repair things when damage is done. Thus in his fatalism Skopas seems once again to come full circle, to Homer.

> Of all creatures that breathe and walk on the earth there is nothing
> More helpless than man is, of all that the earth fosters;
> For he thinks that he will never suffer misfortune in future
> Days, while the gods grant him courage, and his knees have spring
> In them. But when the blessed gods bring sadness upon him,
> Against his will he must suffer it with an enduring spirit.
> For the mind in men upon earth goes according to the fortunes
> The Father of Gods and Men, day by day, bestows upon them.
>
> *Odyssey* xviii. 130–137 (trans. Lattimore)

Skopas
and the Heroic Temper

As the Malibu head so vividly demonstrates, Achilles could be as powerful and soul-stirring a hero in the fourth century as he had ever been. Yet for Skopas' contemporaries the hero par excellence was not the inflexible, wrathful Achilles but Herakles, Telephos' father.[1] Herakles' particular attraction was twofold for, owned by no city in particular, his appeal could be simultaneously international and deeply personal. This was a decided advantage in an age when, as the power of the city-states declined, the growing vigor of inter-city federations, of Macedonian monarchs, and of powerful individuals, all anxious to forward their own "strength relative to the world," was all too plain to see.

The son of Zeus who cleansed the earth of beasts and monsters, Herakles embodies every facet of the human condition in heroic proportions: massively strong yet enthralled to a weakling, virile beyond peer yet active transsexually, wife-defender and wife-murderer, tragic hero and butt of comedy. As Walter Burkert has aptly remarked, "In him the extreme reverts to its opposite, impotence and self-destruction, in order to consolidate itself anew" (Burkert 1977, pp. 322, 323). Such towering humanity earns him in the end what every man hopes for: that final transcendence of mortality in the form of apotheosis among the Olympians, to feast in bliss for eternity. Thus in the works of popular playwrights, thinkers, and rhetoricians Herakles became the paradigm for every man seeking to climb the path to excellence, *areté*, through voluntary submission to toil, *pónos*.[2] These ideas are not new; what is novel is the moralistic emphasis on individual freedom of choice and conscious thought and the happy selection of Herakles as its embodiment.

An early indication of the hero's new role in fourth-century Greek life is to be found in Skopas' early Herakles. Over twenty replicas survive, of which only one is complete: a six-foot (1.76 meter) marble statue presently on loan to the Getty Museum from the Los Angeles County Museum of Art (figs. 6, 49).[3] Identified through a Sikyonian coin image (fig. 50) as Skopas' "stone statue of Herakles in the gymnasium of the agora" (Pausanias, *Description of Greece* II. 10. 1), it was apparently modified somewhat by its Roman copyist. For one thing, the shoulders are abnormally wide, which suggest manufacture for display high on a building. As mentioned above (p. 3), a date for the original of around 370 (toward the beginning of Skopas' career) fits the somewhat tentative and experimental air of the piece as a whole. The shallowness of the skull in profile and the slightly less compressed features also suggest that the piece substantially predates the Tegea sculptures.

The statue showed Herakles holding the Apples of the Hesperides (visible on the coin, fig. 50), earlier brought to him by Atlas while the hero in turn supported the sky on his shoulders. To emphasize Herakles' physical exhaustion, the sculptor boldly abandoned the canonical Polykleitan forms of composition (an especially daring move in Sikyon, the Polykleitan school's second home after Argos) for a posture in which the whole of the right side of the body hangs slackly. Even so, contemporary connoisseurs familiar with Polykleitos' own Herakles (fig. 51)[4] might have recognized the opposition of the relaxed leg and left arm with the apples as an attempt, after Polykleitos, to characterize this arm as "passive"—that is, too weak for any further activity at present. The head turns to follow the gesture, looking off to the spectator's right and helping to establish a relationship between statue and environment.

One can, I think, attempt to be more precise about this relationship and the feelings it was intended to convey to the spectator. By the classical period it seems that the Apples were generally recognized as Herakles' passport to immortality. On several red-figured vases, for instance, he presents them to Zeus in the presence of other deities such as Artemis, Apollo, and Athena.[5] In such pictures the hero is usually, as here, unbearded and young, equipped with club, lionskin, and sometimes a wreath. Since he was actually an old man by this time, the accent on youth and on the variety of attributes must be intentional.

In Skopas' statue, it seems that Herakles' toils (*pónoi*), exemplified by his cauliflowered ears, club, lionskin (representing the first of the Labors), and Apples (the last), as well as by the exhaustion evident in the pose and no doubt to be read into the generalized *páthos* of the face, have at last guaranteed him immortality and eternal youth in heaven. As Pausanias remarks directly after describing Skopas' Herakles, the Sikyonians greatly revered this aspect of him and sacrificed to him as both hero and god.[6] The introduction of this

50. **Herakles on a Sikyonian coin.** Found at Sikyon. Despite the bad condition of the coin, close examination has revealed that the hero's posture and attributes are the same as those of the Hope Herakles, fig. 49. London, British Museum.

49. **The "Hope" Herakles.** Formerly in Deepdene House, England. Only rescued from oblivion quite recently, this copy appears to reproduce Skopas' early statue of Herakles awaiting apotheosis, made for Sikyon: compare the coin on fig. 50. Exhausted by his labors, the rejuvenated hero already shows some of the benefits of the gods' grant of eternal life. Malibu, The J. Paul Getty Museum, on loan from the Los Angeles County Museum of Art, 50.33.22. Original, about 370 B.C.

51. **Herakles by Polykleitos.** Acquired in Rome. This Roman replica of the Herakles by the great fifth-century master Polykleitos is a direct ancestor of Skopas' statue. It should be restored with a club held in the right hand, its thicker end resting on the ground. Rome, Museo Barracco. Original, ca. 440-430 B.C.

practice to Sikyon by the Cretan Phaistos, as Steven   Lattimore has suggested, may even have motivated the inclusion of the bull's head beneath the club—if this is not a Roman addition.

Free choice of the path of *areté* has led Herakles finally to apotheosis, a reward whose guarantee he bears already in his miraculously youthful body, his beardless, rejuvenated features, and the wreath of white poplar bound by a prominently displayed victor's ribbon on his head, his attribute as a god. The Greeks believed that this came from Hades, and that its dual coloring symbolized both life and death, for which reason it was bestowed on Herakles by Pluto when he left the Underworld. As Aristotle said it should, his hair sprouts in short but not too bristly locks straight up from the brow,

48

indicating the leonine character of the hero. By these means Herakles is presented as a role model for the youths of the gymnasium, personifying not only the physical but also the spiritual resources they must cultivate in order to follow even a little way along the path of freely chosen *pónoi* trodden by the greatest of the heroes.

In this statue it is evident that sensitivity to the symbolic content of the hero's attributes and the manner in which they work together with the posture, in order to create patterns (*skhémata*) evocative of distinct moods and situations, is now a basic constituent of the sculptor's art. The spectator must be prepared to "read" such statues as narratives in much the same way as the more explicit arrays of "revelatory" mythology that adorned the attributes of Pheidias' great fifth-century cult statues were "read." Now, however, the narrative lies right at the very heart of the composition, becoming its fundamental premise and organizing principle and locating the statue in a precise framework of space, time, and consequently meaning. Each new attribute, each modification of traditional posture, qualifies this meaning, and all combine to urge the spectator to yet more intense scrutiny of the exact significance of what is presented for his contemplation.

More straightforward, at least at first sight, is the slightly later Lansdowne Herakles, of which about ten replicas survive.[7] Once again, the only near-complete example is in Malibu (figs. 10, 52). It stands just under six-and-one-half feet (1.95 meters) high and is an imposing work indeed. Much of its predecessor's veritable arsenal of attributes has disappeared, with only the lionskin, the club, and a narrow victor's fillet in the hair remaining. The hair itself is still leonine, though less repetitively arranged across the brow; the associations it evokes are strengthened by distinct echoes in the name of the lionskin itself. The skull and general physique are now more developed, and in style it so closely approaches the Tegea fragments (the Malibu head included: figs. 11, 24) that a date in the 350's seems almost mandatory. We do not know where and for whom the original was made, although a very similar Herakles on a slightly later Attic red-figured vase could indicate that it stood in Athens.

A glance at Polykleitos' Doryphoros, or "Spearbearer" (perhaps itself an Achilles), made around 450[8] and now known in about fifty copies (fig. 53), demonstrates not only how much the Lansdowne statue owes to Polykleitos but also how far Skopas has transformed his model to create a new image of the hero.[9] In fact, it is difficult

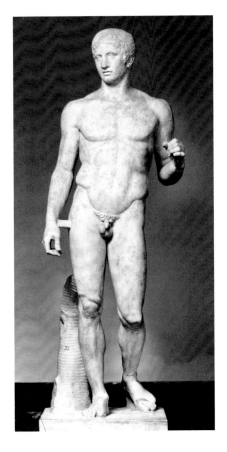

53. The Doryphoros of Polykleitos. From Pompeii. Possibly an Achilles, this paradigm of measured humanity was adopted by many ancient sculptors as a guide for their own art, which they followed "like a law." A massive spear about seven feet long should be restored in the left hand, resting on the shoulder. Naples, Museo Nazionale. Original, about 450-440 B.C.

to escape the suspicion that Skopas intended it to be for the fourth century what Polykleitos' masterpiece had been for the fifth. A powerful and compelling statue, its apparent simplicity is nevertheless born of decidedly complex origins. Like the Doryphoros, it is a polemical statement, a digest of both the traditional and the contemporary, very much concerned with the perennial question of how one defines the essence of heroic *areté* to meet the needs of a changing world.

52. The Lansdowne Herakles. From Hadrian's Villa at Tivoli, then in Lansdowne House, London. An imposing statue, this Herakles copies a lost work of Skopas showing the hero after his fight with the lion, facing the future and all that it holds in store for him. Malibu, The J. Paul Getty Museum. Original, about 360-350 B.C.

51

In contrast to the "mobile repose" of the Doryphoros, the Lansdowne Herakles simply stands. The sculptor has taken over a posture long established in the Polykleitan school and pushed it to extremes. The supposedly "relaxed" left leg is now set so far out that the weight of the torso rests upon it almost as heavily as it does upon the right, a feeling confirmed by the compression of the left hip muscles. This shift from a straightforward antithesis between weight-bearing and free-to-varying degrees of muscular tension is carried into the arms, where the supposedly relaxed right arm carries the lionskin, a burden only slightly lighter, one imagines, than the club in the left. The head is raised and turned to its left, as before, but now unites with the diagonals of the club and left leg to unlock the classical "closed" stance completely for the first time. Meanwhile a solid wall of verticals closes off the other side, providing a firm foundation from which this bold projection into space may develop. The left shoulder is slightly withdrawn, easing the transition between the torso and proudly erect head, while a slow, serpentine curve (maybe derived ultimately from Praxiteles) passes up through the body, unifying it and distancing the play of weight and muscular response ever so slightly from one's normal human reaction to gravity and its demands.

Set a little apart from ordinary humanity in this way and well over life-size compared with the average Greek male, Herakles stands foursquare and rocklike. His steadfastness is firmly rooted in his past achievements, represented by the lionskin, testimony to his first Labor, in his right hand; yet by gazing far into the distance he also seems to challenge the future, as it lies before him. The spectator, manipulated by the relative flatness and sheer breadth of the composition into standing directly opposite the front of the plinth, seems to eavesdrop on a narrative in the making. Herakles simply ignores him, gazing resolutely out toward the horizon where his destiny lies, creating an aura of heroic endeavor to come. Ordinary men have no place in this world: we may ponder, even strive to emulate, but not approach.

So where the Doryphoros of Polykleitos proclaimed even down to its smallest detail the paradigmatic role of the ever-ready hero, measured of both physique and temper, in the context of an ordered universe the Lansdowne Herakles asserts something of a contrary ideal. *Areté* for him is fixity of purpose: his choices seem over and done with.

Even so, it is intriguing to note that whereas the eyes of the Sikyon Herakles were turned a little upward (presumably toward Olympos), here they look down slightly. This occurs on some of the other copies, and could suggest a more introspective character than might be imagined at first sight. One recalls the thinking, calculating Herakles of the late fifth- and early fourth-century writers, sensible "to what man is worth."[10] Such practical wisdom or *phrónesis,* combined with endurance, an indomitable will, and unflinching devotion to duty (once determined) are now fully established as the prime essentials for the true hero. The categorically ideal Polykleitan image with its implication of absolute freedom of action is no longer viable in such a world; instead, the hero must think and battle continuously to maintain even what he has. It is at this point that one should look forward to both Telephos and Achilles (figs. 45, 46) in the Tegea pediment.

In fact Euripides, writing two generations earlier in the middle of the ruinous Peloponnesian War (431–404), had already set the tone for this conception of the heroic (and for much of fourth-century experience besides) when he had Theseus declare to Herakles, and Herakles himself accept, that:

> Who of men is noble in spirit,
> Bears the blows of heaven, and flinches not.
> *The Madness of Herakles,* 1227–28

The power of Skopas' vision of the heroic enterprise is perhaps evidenced by the many fourth-century Hellenistic and Roman Herakles types eclectically dependent on these two statues.[11] Given what appears to have been the widespread acceptance of his work as a definitive statement about the nature of truly heroic *areté,* it may be revealing to compare Skopas' third great hero statue, the Meleager, against it (figs. 19, 20, 54).[12]

The Meleager, known from over forty copies and popular in Roman times for conversion to portraiture, was a work of truly heroic scale, almost seven feet (2.10 meters) high. Of the ten more-or-less complete replicas, the dog and cloak are present in most (although the fluttering drapery of the Vatican copy is surely a copyist's fantasy), the boar's head in three, and the rock only in the Vatican statue (fig. 54). A high-quality variant in the Fogg Art Museum (fig. 19) substitutes a staff or short lance wedged under the armpit for the great boar-spear and apparently drapes the cloak over the left fore-

54. Meleager. From Rome. This replica shows the hero Meleager after the hunt of the Kalydonian boar and before the conflicts over the division of the spoils, which were to lead to his own death. The fluttering end of the cloak is a copyist's addition, as may be the rock and boar's head. Rome, Vatican Museums. Original, about 340 B.C. or shortly thereafter.

arm only. Since it was found in a Roman villa together with a Meleager of more orthodox type (now in Berlin), it is perhaps safest to assume that these unique modifications were ordered by the nameless Roman collector who commissioned it. The original location of Skopas' statue is unknown. Comparison with the Getty head (figs. 24, 57) secures the attribution beyond reasonable doubt, and indicates that it was made late in the sculptor's career, perhaps shortly after 340.

The statue shows the hero Meleager after his triumph in the Kalydonian hunt, but before his generosity in giving the head and hide of the boar to Atalante led to the fight in which he killed his uncles Prothoos and Kometes, who also claimed the prize. Grief-stricken for her brothers, his mother then burned the torch to which Meleager's life was tied and so killed him in requital. The hero's choice, the path of *areté,* is no longer straightforward, and it is to this dilemma between love or kinship that the whole composition seems to be attuned.

As with the Lansdowne Herakles, reminiscences of Polykleitos' Doryphoros (fig. 53) are prominent, especially in the stance and the positioning of the spear. Polykleitos' Herakles (fig. 51), too, might have suggested the attitude of the right arm. Yet as before, the sculptor quotes his predecessor only to demonstrate in the next breath how differently his own hero is placed relative to his world. Meleager has none of the easy freedom of the Doryphoros and lacks even the trenchant determination of the Lansdowne Herakles. Instead, the uncompromising vertical of the great spear now closes the statue's left side almost completely, while the swaying stance with its serpentine axis, undulant muscles, and slow twist of the body in the opposite direction to the turn of the head suggest a character at once more labile and less steadfast than the Herakles—though not yet the doubt-riven antihero of Hellenistic epic, such as Jason in Apollonios' *Argonautica*, written about 250. Meleager no longer stands foursquare to face the world as Herakles did. His posture is more equivocal, as he looks out toward the future while physically turning away from it.

Once again, the indeterminate *páthos* of the features (cf. fig. 20) no doubt allowed the spectator to read a similar conflict in the face: the expression seems anxious now, yet the mask is still composed and heroic. Meleager may indeed have killed the boar, but even in the moment of triumph, as in Euripides' *Meleager*, he is burdened with the perils ahead. We are reminded of what he may already suspect (but cannot know for sure)—that the spoils he has won will cause dispute and bloodshed, and may eventually be fatal. The spectator is now invited to participate in the hero's mental processes in a much stronger way, to ponder the choice before him and his wisdom (*phrónesis*) or otherwise in resolving it, and perhaps even to meditate on the lesson of the whole saga as expressed in Euripides' concluding line, "how quickly a god reverses prosperity" (*Meleager* fr. 536 Nauck). The frustration of both Telephos and Achilles at the climax of the Kaikos fight (fig. 45, 46) comes immediately to mind.

Yet despite Skopas' subtle and penetrating psychological insight, one is still kept somewhat at a distance by the classical aloofness of the pose and by the strictly controlled features that, as at Tegea, prevent the *páthos* of the situation from becoming particularized. As G. M. A. Hanfmann writes, "The Meleager represents the last stage in which the increasing diversification of movement and the individuation of the *persona* could still be contained within a typical posture derived from the classic tradition.... [He] is still primarily the courageous, defiant, tragic hero, and not an individual displaying those qualities" (Hanfmann 1964, p. 65).

With the Meleager we reach the end of Skopas' personal contribution to the evolution of the image of the hero in late classical Greece. Appropriately, for a society weakening both politically and spiritually, it was an image increasingly full of doubt and unease. Yet it would be idle to end here, for at this point the story is only half told. What of Skopas' influence, particularly over his apparently longer-lived contemporary Lysippos, both in the special genre of hero statues and in the portraiture of their latter-day successor, Alexander the Great?

Beyond Skopas

From the literary and other evidence, it was apparently Lysippos who played the leading role in interpreting the characters of heroes, both mythical and historical, for the later fourth century.[1] No fewer than five statues of Herakles and one free-standing group of the entire cycle of Twelve Labors are recorded in the sources, for locations ranging from Italy to Macedon. The only one that concerns us directly here, however, is a Weary Herakles grasping the apples in his right hand, known in a large number of versions but very few true copies.[2] The Getty Museum owns four such derivations: a Roman ivory statuette (fig. 55), two small Roman bronzes, and a small Renaissance marble. Together with a fine Roman bronze in the Louvre (fig. 56) they give an excellent idea of the original composition. Since the statue was depicted on the silver coins of Sikyon by the end of the fourth century,[3] it seems possible that it was the work by Lysippos seen by Pausanias in the agora there, near Skopas' Herakles. Most critics accept a date late in Lysippos' career for it, say about 320.

The likely location of the Weary Herakles in Sikyon encourages the suspicion that it is attempting to better Skopas' earlier try at the same theme (fig. 49). Lysippos was evidently a contentious personality: his Eros at Thespiae was apparently another such riposte, this time to Praxiteles.[4] The choice once again of the return with the Apples certainly fits the Sikyonians' unusual preoccupation with this aspect of the hero's life, although significant alterations in almost every aspect of the presentation testify to Lysippos' concern to beat Skopas at his own game.

Unlike Skopas' Herakles, Lysippos' is old and exhausted, lacking any attributes of victory save his club and lionskin and any symbols of apotheosis save the Apples themselves, held as if forgotten behind his back and invisible to the casual spectator. As yet unaware of his impending reward and untouched by its promise of eternal youth, he stands in a pose eloquent of utter exhaustion, leaning sluggishly on his club and lionskin and looking down at the tokens of his toils.

Like Polykleitos a century earlier (fig. 51), Lysippos exploits the viewer's expectations about the cross-relationships of arms and legs in order to increase the general impression of overwhelming fatigue. The left arm, nominally "engaged" since it is opposite to the

55, 56. The Weary Herakles of Lysippos. Two replicas, one of unknown provenance, the other (fig. 56) from Northern Italy. In this "improvement" upon the Hope Herakles, Lysippos depicts the hero as ironically unaware of the results of his acquisition of the Apples of the Hesperides (held behind his back): eternal life in bliss among the immortals. Fig. 55: Malibu, The J. Paul Getty Museum. Fig. 56: Paris, Louvre. Original, about 320 B.C.

supporting leg (compare the Lansdowne Herakles, fig. 52), hangs down loosely over the club, while the right, nominally "relaxed," lazily angles back behind the hip as if to imitate the Polykleitan Herakles and the Meleager (figs. 51, 54), but this time the hand actually grasps the Apples. By this literal sleight of hand Lysippos dupes the spectator into accepting that the right arm is even weaker than the other. When he has swallowed the bait but perhaps wishes to make doubly sure, the sculptor then paradoxically confronts him with the true reason why—the Apples and the toil (*pónos*) he has endured to get them.

Lysippos' statue, then, sought to magnify the hero's impending apotheosis by magnifying (in unanticipated and therefore doubly telling fashion) the *pónoi* by which he earned it. The mighty physique that endowed Herakles with the strength to surmount all trials has barely mastered this, his final task. Utterly spent by what seems to have been only a pyrrhic victory, heedless, like the casual spectator, of the Apples that will be his salvation, this aging, worn-out strongman has apparently reached a total dead end.

Yet with its contemplative, intelligent expression, the head perhaps hints at a deeper level to the hero's character: namely, the tremendous spiritual gifts that now constituted his prime claim to *areté* without peer. To this view, greatness of soul and superlative strength reinforce one another to create in Herakles a true paragon of heroism, here ironically portrayed as still unaware of his coming reward. Unlike Skopas, Lysippos leaves this leap of faith entirely to the spectator, inviting, almost compelling him, through the concealment of the Apples, to share his hero's desolation to the end.

The Weary Herakles, it seems, thus brought together all previous ideas of what constituted the true *aretaí* of Herakles, his real claim to apotheosis and everlasting honor and glory: the Homeric, with its emphasis on his gigantic prowess; the tragic, with its stress on unflinching endurance regardless of circumstances; and the philosophic, with its accent on greatness of spirit. Not the least of this statue's many ironies is that (as the philosophers had already recognized) with the Labors completed, the great body that triumphed over all Fate and Chance could do to it is now an encumbrance, a prison rather than an asset. The weakness of Herakles' own mortal flesh, magnified with his body to more than human scale, chains him to earth and distracts him, as it does us, from what really matters: the Apples and their promise of heaven.

Not only in demand all over the Greek world for his bronzes of gods and heroes, Lysippos was engaged by Alexander in the 330's to be his court portraitist.[5] From the ancient sources and from the meager material remains, it is clear that these statues of the king were at once an end—the consummation of the heroic tradition in classical Greek sculpture—and a new beginning—an affirmation of the ancient belief that heroes would one day walk the earth again.

Alexander, who became king of Macedon in 336 at the age of twenty, was well placed to usher in this new heroic age, being descended on his father's side from Herakles and on his mother's from Achilles. As his biographer Plutarch remarked, "This is accepted without question" (*Alexander* II. 1).

Alexander's emulation of Herakles is a constant motif among the historians, who often allude to the whole eastern campaign as a latter-

57. The Malibu head. This photograph of the head of Achilles introduces a number of later fourth-century images of heroes, either dependent upon Skopas or conceived in a spirit of rivalry with his work.

day repetition of that hero's own expedition to India. As for his interest in Achilles, this was apparent from boyhood.[6] Lysimachos, his tutor before Aristotle, played up to it by dubbing himself "Phoenix," Alexander "Achilles," and Philip "Peleus." The *Iliad,* too, became his pupil's bible, which he reportedly kept under his pillow. Landing in Asia in 334, Alexander made straight for Troy, where he and his lifelong companion, Hephaistion, sacrificed to Achilles and Patroklos, respectively. Visiting the temple of Athena, he saw the armor of the Achaian heroes inside and exchanged some of his own for it. Significantly, he wore this armor at the battle of the Granikos a week or two later. As the march eastward continued and success followed success, so were his court poets and historians increasingly swept up by the heroic mystique of their dashing, intensely charismatic young leader, with his leonine hair, arresting glance, handsome features, and fearless, driving energy. Choirilos wrote an epic after the *Iliad,* predictably casting his patron in the role of Achilles, and Kallisthenes produced a nauseatingly sycophantic biography in prose that did the same.

Not surprisingly, then, when Lysippos turned to creating his bronzes of Alexander, he showed him nude and holding the great heroic lance of Achilles, a latter-day Doryphoros for a new heroic age. Alexander's enthusiasm was immediate:

58. **Alexander the Great.** Said to be from Tivoli. This copy of a Lysippic bronze shows Alexander as the new Achilles, rivalling Skopas' image of the all-powerful, all-conquering hero. Vienna, Schwarzenberg collection. Original, 334-323 B.C.

Lysippos alone, he thought, expressed his character in the bronze and in its forms displayed his *areté*. Others who strove to imitate the turn of his neck and the limpidity and moistness of his eyes failed to do justice to his virile and leonine character.

Plutarch, *On the Fortune of Alexander,* II. 2. 335B

In contrast to the relatively informative nature of the written tradition, preserved fourth-century Alexander portraits or faithful copies of them are very few indeed (figs. 58, 62). Lysippos' bronzes have all disappeared, and Roman sensitivity to the whole question of universal monarchy and its possible abuse (for which Alexander later became a by-word) meant that replicas were liable to be conceived from a decidedly partisan viewpoint.

A well-preserved head in Vienna (fig. 58) is the finest of these replicas, and once again seems to demonstrate Lysippos' very equivocal relationship to Skopas' hero, as represented by the Malibu head. As in the Skopaic work, many of the signs of the leonine nature are present—the square-proportioned face, the high forehead, the rather deep-set eyes, "neither very round nor very narrow," and particularly the full mane of hair cascading down from the back-combed, central parting or *anastolé* (compare the Lansdowne Herakles, figs. 10, 52). Yet the features are finer, tauter, and immediately more individual, especially the mouth, than in the

Skopaic piece. Even in the copy we can sense that this is a real, living man, a unique person who is at the same time ideal and a hero, too.

As Plutarch tells us, in the original it was particularly through the "moist" and "limpid" eyes that this heroic charisma of Alexander's, this personal magnetism that drew his followers after him almost to the ends of the earth, found its outlet and true expression. In the ancient world many believed that the eyes actually exuded light rather than simply reflected it, and that "moist" eyes (especially characteristic of the young) enabled the light from within to shine more brightly upon the world. Empedokles and Plato both subscribed to this theory, and Polemon, head of the Platonic Academy in the early third century, even wrote that "eyes that are moist shine like torches and best reveal the characters of men" (*Anecdota Graeca* ed. Cramer, IV. 255). Alexander's tutor Aristotle, however, preferred to believe that such "moistness" enabled the eyes to *receive* more light; "limpidity," that other feature of Alexander's eyes caught by Lysippos, was to him a function of this "moistness," helping the light to traverse the pupil unobstructed and thus aiding clarity of sight.[7] Yet whatever were the opinions of monarch and sculptor, it is clear that Alexander's eyes, full of life and energy, lustrous and light-filled, were the key to much of his hold over his contemporaries. In the bronze, Lysippos will have taken particular care to heighten this feature, perhaps by increasing the reflectivity of the inlay used for the pupils. To do justice to this most characteristic of Alexander's features would have been impossible for a marble-carver like Skopas.

In his Alexander portraits, then, Lysippos seems to have been less concerned with making universal, a priori statements or with an objectively realistic portrayal of the king's actual physiognomy,[8] than with satisfying the viewer's preconceptions of the nature of Alexander's character, heroic affiliations, and place in history. Molding the opinions of the uncommitted or even perhaps the actively hostile must have come a close second. So whereas earlier portraitists had either begun with an ideal type (Herakles or Achilles) and personalized it to a greater or lesser extent, or had attempted a more-or-less straightforward realism, Lysippos began with reality (Alexander's own physiognomy) and subtly *idealized* it. Indeed, his portraits are perhaps the earliest in Greek art to which this term, in its strict sense, may properly be applied. So, as he himself said, "whereas his predecessors had represented men as they were [in essence? in reality?], he represented them as they appeared to be." (Pliny, *Natural*

59. "Ares Ludovisi." From Italy. This brooding, intense image of the god of war copies a statue made by a close follower of Skopas. Not surprisingly, he seems to have taken Skopas' image of the most warlike of the heroes as his point of departure. Rome, Museo Nazionale delle Terme. Original, about 330 B.C.

60. Head of "Ares Ludovisi" type. Perhaps from Italy. A replica once of superb quality, this head even in its ruin shows something of the Skopaic proportions and deep-set eyes favored by the sculptor of the original statue. Malibu, The J. Paul Getty Museum. Original, about 330 B.C.

History XXXIV, 65). In his Alexander-Achilles, then, he sought to trump Skopas' achievement, by using it as his point of departure, yet at the same time decisively recasting it to fit the needs of the new age of unfettered individualism that dawned with the great crusade to the east.

While in Alexander portraiture it was clearly the Lysippic approach that had momentarily gained the advantage, in contemporary images of Achilles as well as the many eclectic Herakles statues mentioned earlier, the reverse seems to have been true. The famous seated "Ares Ludovisi" (figs. 59, 60)[9]—maybe originally an Achilles but in any case a work of brooding, powerful intensity—was probably made in the 330's. The Getty Museum already possesses several replicas of widely varying fidelity; these and others show that the statue was closely

dependent on Skopas in many respects. A new copy of excellent quality but now sadly battered, also in the museum (fig. 60), strengthens the relationship—the heavy chin, deep-set eyes, and powerful, "clouded" brow are all there.

An even closer kinship exists between the de Bry head and the head of Achilles from a fresco in Herculaneum showing him at a music lesson with Cheiron the Centaur (fig. 61).[10] The date of the original painting may lie within the fourth century, although the matter is complicated by the existence in antiquity of a sculptured group of the same type in Rome which was probably much later. Although the question of priority may never be settled, the strength of the Skopaic tradition in the copy remains undeniable.

The existence of another anti-Lysippic (or at least non-Lysippic) tradition is evident in certain "heroic" portraits of Alexander created after his death. A prime document for such trends is the Getty Alexander, acquired in 1972 and one of the prizes of the museum's collection (fig. 62).[11] Despite the staunch opposition of the traditionalists in Athens and elsewhere, cults of Alexander were already springing up by the time of his death in 323.[12] His burial, mummified, in a sumptuous tomb at Alexandria shortly after 320, represents a further stage in what has rightly been called his removal from reality. This period sees not only a tendency to transfer faith in the traditional gods to divinely-inspired humans, but also the earliest attempts by various interested parties to reinterpret Alexander's career in partisan terms. The Getty head, a masterpiece of marble carving from the very end of the century, bears striking witness to these new developments.

The set of sculptures to which it belongs, perhaps originally from Greece, seems to have been displayed inside an architectural framework with akroteria (apples, pomegranates, and birds) of a distinctly funerary cast. Besides the Alexander, the group includes a head of Hephaistion, a sensitive head of a woman (maybe a princess), a head of a flute-player, and fragments of other figures making sacrifice. The Alexander and Hephaistion both wore crowns, indicating that they were almost certainly dead at the time (Hephaistion died in October

61. **Achilles learns the lyre.** From the Basilica, Herculaneum. The young Achilles, learning the lyre from his mentor Cheiron, is swept up by the beauty of its music. Once more, Skopas' own Achilles is a prime component of the image. Naples, Museo Nazionale. Original, perhaps ca. 330-300 B.C.

62. The Getty Alexander. Alexander, from a multi-figured group set in an architectural frame, mourns for the dead Hephaistion as Achilles once mourned for Patroklos. Malibu, The J. Paul Getty Museum. About 320-300 B.C.

324, nine months before Alexander). One might imagine that the whole may have functioned as the cenotaph of some central or northern Greek princess, in which Alexander and Hephaistion were included to bolster family prestige and link it with the cult of the king and his companion.

Whatever the truth may be, the romanticized pathos of the Alexander with its tense, mobile flesh, strong features, upward glance, and trembling, undulating lips is immediately striking. The rejuvenation of the king, now of course a god, recalls the rejuvenated head of the Sikyon Herakles (figs. 6, 7, 49). Indeed, there is much that is Skopaic in the rendering too, although it is now translated into a new idiom of nervous dynamism and tragic longing. The *anastolé* apart, from Lysippos there is virtually nothing.

It is a sobering thought that until recently an immediate connection would probably have been made between this head and the famous motif of Alexander's *póthos*.[13] This is retailed by his biographer Arrian (ca. A.D. 96–180) and was once eloquently interpreted as a "longing for the unattainable, for things not, or no longer within reach, the motive force of the conqueror of the world" (Ehrenberg 1938, p. 60). The head's obvious indebtedness to Skopas' Pothos (fig. 21) for several elements of its formal vocabulary would no doubt have been cited as confirmation. Yet, in fact, *póthos* in Arrian has no such high-flown tragic drama attached to it, and never motivates any major move on Alexander's part. Rather, it is simply a convenient formula to describe the king's curiosity in seeing interesting places and things, normally with only a few companions at his side.

A more plausible explanation for the evident emotionalism of the piece may perhaps be found in the tenor of the writings of his court historians, whose accounts must have circulated in Greece during his last years and after his death. Specifically, one thinks of the pseudo-heroic accounts of Choirilos and Kallisthenes and of the historical fact of Alexander's overwhelming grief at Hephaistion's death. The parallel of Achilles' grief for Patroklos (*Iliad* XVIII.22-27, XXIII.12-23) would, in such circumstances, have been too close to ignore. With due caution one may, therefore, offer this motif as an aid to interpreting the monument, which was itself perhaps erected in a similar atmosphere of grief for a departed loved one.

At any rate, to co-opt Alexander for such ends as these, whether propagandistic or exemplary or both, takes us a decisive step into the Hellenistic age, toward the Alexander of legend rather than fact.

The crown that once circled his head shows that here he has passed beyond the realm of the human, even of the heroic, to that of the divine. By this time Skopas was, one assumes, long dead, and although his influence was strong in early Hellenistic ruler portraits,[14] they are beyond the limits of this discussion. It is time to return to the de Bry head itself.

Retrospect

Clearly, the Getty head and the ensemble to which it belonged occupied a crucial position in Skopas' oeuvre and in the evolution of the late classical image of the hero. By suggesting a wider perspective for the head than the confines of a small town in provincial Arkadia, the last two sections indicate that a rapid reappraisal of Skopas' achievement at Tegea may be a convenient means of closing this discussion.

It is often said that one of the most fertile ways to consider a work of art is as a solution to compound problems. At Tegea, the situation that Skopas faced was more complex than usual in fourth-century sculpture, in that it involved problems (some of a more general cast and some peculiar to that particular commission) of a political, religious, intellectual, and even socioeconomic character. Prominent among these seem to have been the need to create a new sense of the status and worth of the heroic enterprise; to respond to contemporary notions of the way heroes look and behave under stress; to present in a convincing and vivid way a tricky plot in which locals had a very large axe to grind; and to steer clear of the academic formalism of the Polykleitan school on the one hand and the well-bred reserve of the Attic on the other. Finally, the sculptor had to manage and perhaps even train under difficult circumstances a large workshop for rapid and trouble-free production of about forty life-size marble statues and twelve-meter-square metopes, not to mention probably a further narrative in high relief on the altar.[1]

Skopas' solution, or rather his response to these conditions, involved the refinement of a style of great sculptural power, characterized by a relative uniformity of detail, a certain indeterminacy of pathos, and a dramatic turn of narrative. To a great extent problem and solution, conditions and response, may be seen to match, but not in the sense of a directly reciprocal connection between this particular circumstance and that particular contrivance. Thus, the exigencies of large-scale workshop production did not, in themselves, create the general uniformity of detail observable on the pedimental heads, any more than did the sculptor's desire to regularize the presentation of the hero or to contain his emotions within acceptable bounds. Not only are such differentiating explanations inherently unlikely, since an artist's style necessarily evolves over a longer period of time and in response to a wider set of circumstances than those bounded by a single commission, but Skopas by all evidence did not possess the calculatingly analytic mind of a Polykleitos or a Lysippos. Rather, it is a measure of the sureness of his intuition that at Tegea his ability to adapt to changing conditions called forth a performance that, taken in aggregate, matches the sum of his problems, an integrating solution that corresponds to the entirety of his circumstances.

The Malibu head now reveals to us, for the very first time, the heights that such a solution could attain. Although we will never be absolutely sure that it was carved by Skopas himself, a direct attribution of this kind is in a sense irrelevant. What matters is that its quality and power suffice to place it at the forefront of all surviving architectural marbles of the late classic period. In its unequaled command of both the generalized vocabulary of the heroic ideal and the subtle particulars of human response to circumstance, it speaks to us across the centuries as hardly less than a work of genius. Unless one is obsessed with names, there is no point in asking for more.

Appendix I:
Skin Textures and the Pseudo-Aristotelian Physiognomica

As was explained on pp. 32-33, late classical Greek had developed a fairly extensive set of terms to describe the texture of human skin, a matter also of consuming interest to sculptors. Something of the complexity of their thinking on the matter may be conveyed by a survey of the pseudo-Aristotelian *Physiognomica,* compiled from the work of Aristotle's pupils at the beginning of the third century B.C. For convenience, many of the terms used in this treatise may be grouped schematically into a table of opposites.

sarkódes	fleshy	*ásarkos*	fleshless
eúsarkos	well-fleshed		
euektikós	wholesome		
húgros	moist, supple	*xerós*	dry
		aukhmerós	dry
hapalós	soft, yielding	*skléros*	hard
malakós	soft	*stereós*	firm
leíos	smooth	*rhutidódes*	wrinkled
apoleluménos	slack	*sundedeménos*	tight-knit
eulútos	relaxed	*prosestalménos*	tight-drawn
laparós	loose		
khalarós	slack, loose		
pimelódes	fatty	*iskhnós*	lean, spare
píon	fat, rich	*leptós*	thin, delicate

The translations are approximate only, though for that very reason the greater sensitivity of the Greek is clear. Also, they do no justice to the subtler, value-laden connotations of these terms. Thus the *Physiognomonica* informs us that "flesh which is *skléros* and naturally *euektikós* signifies lack of sensibility, while that which is *leíos* shows a pleasant but unstable character, unless it occurs in a strong body having powerful extremities" (2. 806b22). All this, too, does not touch the related and equally complex matter of skin *color*, which receives a separate section to itself in chapter 6 of the Aristotelian treatise.

Of course, such sensitivity, presumably sharpened by everyday acquaintance with all sorts of nude male bodies at the gymnasium, has roots far back in Greek culture. Homer occasionally shows awareness of surface textures, and by the fifth century the more analytical of the classical authors could produce quite sophisticated personal descriptions along these lines. It was the fourth century, however, alive to the usefulness of such observations both for medical diagnosis and for character analysis, that applied itself systematically to the question. This research, by Aristotle and others, laid the groundwork for what was soon to become an important sub-branch of the science of physiognomics. The relevance of yet other branches of this science toward an appreciation of the expressive subtleties of the head was explored in the pages on the Wrath of Achilles, pp. 42-43.

Concerning skin textures, however, we are two-and-a-half millennia too late to appreciate the fine distinctions that the Aristotelian writers offer us, and we can only guess at their exact significance for late classical sculptors. It is tempting, for instance, to characterize the face of the Antikythera youth as somewhat "tight-drawn," while the Aberdeen head in contrast appears "supple," even "moist," and the Getty head perhaps "well-fleshed" and "smooth." Yet nuances of the kind which we encounter especially in these last two pieces are delicate and do not respond well to assault with a catalogue of terms, particularly when (as now) these are only half understood at best. It would seem better for the present to leave conclusions unstated and allow the sculpture, thus prompted, to speak for itself. Also, as the physiognomer himself warns us, "It is foolish to put one's faith in any single characteristic" (*Physiognomonica* 2. 806b38).

Appendix II:

The Tegean Building Contract

(The following text is translated from the inscription as published in Hiller von Gaertringen 1913, no. 6.)

Concerning Te[gean public works and procedures in the event of dis]putes.

(1) If any trouble arises between contractors on the same work, as regards the work: the injured party shall prosecute the offender within three days from the time the offense was committed, but no later; and whatever the managing committee decides shall be binding.

(2) If war should interrupt any of the works contracted for or should destroy any of those completed, the Three Hundred shall determine what must be done. The generals shall furnish revenue, if it seems to them that it is war that is hindering or has destroyed the works, after holding a sale of booty in the city. But if anyone who has made a contract has not begun on the works and war interrupts, he shall return whatever money he may have received and be excused from the work, if the managing committee so orders.

(3) If anyone combines to oppose the allocation of the works or does an injury in any way, the managing committee shall impose whatever penalty they think fit, and shall proclaim it for trial and bring it to the court constituted to fix the amount of the penalty.

(4) More than two partners are forbidden for any one piece of work; if this is disobeyed, let each owe fifty drachmas, and let the heliasts impose the fine. Anyone who wishes may be informer, receiving half the fine as a reward. And also, if any contractor undertakes more than two pieces of either sacred or public work, in any manner for which the heliasts have not posted their unanimous consent, he shall be fined fifty drachmas per month for each piece of excess work, until all the excess pieces of work cease.

(5) If any[one is a liti]gant concerning any of the te[rms of the contract] for the works, he shall n[ot receive pa]y; otherwise, he shall not have the right of trial elsewhere than at Tegea; and if he is sued, he shall pay double the amount for which the suit is brought. And the same person who was the guarantor for the work shall stand

surety for the payment of this fine.

(6) If a contractor injures any of the existing works, whether sacred, public, or private, contrary to the terms of this contract, he must at his own expense put it in as good condition as it was at the time of the contract. But if he does not make good the damage, he must pay the same penalties that are fixed for other pieces of work overdue.

(7) If a contractor or workman seems to be abusing the works, or to be disobedient to those in charge, or disregardful of the established fines, the workman may be expelled from the work, and the contractor brought to trial and fined in the same way as has been prescribed for those who make opposition to the allocations.

(8) Whenever any sacred or public work is allocated, this general contract shall be in force in addition to the special contract for the particular piece of work.

(Lists of disbursements and fines then follow against the names of the various contractors, but no contracts themselves are recorded. These must have been written down elsewhere, on stone or papyrus, and have subsequently perished. Lines 59–62 and 70–73, however, mention payments of prize money from the treasurers of the generals to the yearly college of magistrates (*epieteîai*). Clause 2 in the contract must therefore have come into force, suggesting that at this time war—presumably with Sparta—did indeed interrupt or threaten to interrupt the work. Numerous sources indeed testify to continual raids across the border between 362 and 338, and tell of at least one major Spartan expedition into Arkadia in the same period.)

Notes

(Authors' names refer to the bibliography; all abbreviations of journal titles, etc., are as prescribed in the *American Journal of Archaeology* 82 [1978] 3–10.)

Preface
Previous accounts of the head of Achilles, sometimes called the de Bry head, (inv. 79.AA. 7) are to be found in Chamoux 1979, XV-XVII; Frel 1979, 6; 1980, 90–93; Chamoux 1981, 1–16; Vermeule 1981 no. 50.

The Man and His Work
1. On Skopas' life and works see Stewart 1977, passim; reviews: Chamoux 1979b, 564–65; Lattimore 1978, 415–16; Palagia 1979, 212–113; Ridgway 1980, 114–15; Stupperich 1980, 280–85; Vafopoulou-Richardson 1979, 117–118.
2. Aristandros: Pausanias III. 18.8; Stewart 1977, 127 no. 2.
3. Herakles at Sikyon: Stewart 1977, 90–91, 130 no. 27 (Pausanias II. 10. 1), 139–40, pls. 30–31, 52; Lattimore 1975, 17–21, figs. 1–5 (with excellent discussion of the iconography, superseding my own in *Skopas of Paros*); Howard 1978, 29–30, figs. 86–89; Vermeule 1981, no. 49; Vierneisel-Schlörb 1979, 307 n. 15 prefers to see this statue as a pastiche.
4. Aphrodite Pandemos: Stewart 1977, 93, 127 no. 3 (Pausanias VI. 25.1), 141, pl. 33a; add now Lattimore 1976, 53–54, who shows that the list of the replicas should be restricted yet further.
5. Tegea: Stewart 1977, 5–84, 133 no. 36 (Pausanias VIII. 45. 4–7), figs. 2–5, pls. 1–23, 52; on the architecture of the temple see Dugas 1924, passim; suggested revisions in the reconstruction of the interior, Norman 1980, 225.
6. Maenad: Stewart 1977, 91–93, 130–31 (*Anthologia Planudea* 60; *Anthologia Palatina* IX. 774; Callistratus, *Statuarum descriptiones* II), 140–41, pl. 32; Stupperich 1980, 283–84 rightly objects that in my analysis of this and the Pothos I paid too much attention to the "formal imperative" and too little to the motif and subject as an explanation for the differences in Skopas' handling of torsion and *contrapposto* in each. Despite this, however, I still feel that the Amazon of Mausoleum slab 1014 could hardly have been conceived without prior knowledge of the Maenad, and therefore prefer to maintain a rather earlier dating for her than others are wont to accept.
7. Lansdowne Herakles: Stewart 1977, 98–99, 142, 147, pls. 42, 52; Howard 1978, passim; Vermeule 1981 no. 54; cf. Lattimore 1975, 21–26, figs. 6–10 (rebutted on methodological grounds by Vierneisel-Schlörb 1979, 307 n. 15); on the particular closeness of the Lansdowne and Malibu heads see already Frel 1980, 92 n. 8, as against, e.g., Palagia 1979, 213.
8. Apollo: Stewart 1977, 93–94, 127–28 nos. 6–8 (Pliny, *N.H.* XXXVI. 25; Propertius II. 31.15; *Notitia: descriptio urbis Romae*, Regio X), 141–42 and addendum p. 151; pl. 33b. cf. Lattimore 1976, 6 n. 2, where it is dated to ca. 370, but as with my own problems concerning the Maenad, this perhaps pays too little attention to the dictates of the subject in determining posture and rhythm. Clearly, as far as concerns the fourth

century at least, formal analysis alone is an insufficient and maybe even actively misleading way to construct a chronology.

9. The Mausoleum: Stewart 1977, 95–98, 132 nos. 34–35 (Pliny, *Natural History* XXXVI. 30–31; Vitruvius VII. praef. 13), pls. 34–41; Waywell 1978, passim; excellent discussion in Hornblower 1982, ch. 9; after Cook 1976, 52–53, pl. 6f, the torso and head attached to BM 1012 figure 47 (Stewart 1977, pls. 34, 35a, 37a) should now definitely be disregarded as alien to this slab.

10. On Skopas' Asian work other than at the Mausoleum see Stewart 1977, 95–103, 111–12, 128–32 nos. 13, 17, 21, 33 (Pliny, *Natural History* XXXVI. 22 and 95; Strabo XIII. 604 and XIV. 640). The Smintheum itself is evidently mid Hellenistic or later; on its sculptured drums, which look late to me, see most recently Bingöl 1980, 257—64.

11. Marine Thiasos: Stewart 1977, 99–101, 132 no. 32 (Pliny, *Natural History* XXXVI. 26), pl. 43; and now Lattimore 1976, passim.

12. Ada-Idreus relief: Smith 1916, 65–70, fig. 1. Other carvers at Tegea may have been native Peloponnesians: Linfert 1966, 28–32, 39–40 and others have already noted affiliations between one of the helmeted heads (Stewart 1977, 24 no. 18, pl. 16) and Peloponnesian work. Interestingly, this is among the least satisfactory of all the surviving heads from the temple: might its sculptor have been an addition to the workshop, trained in a hurry to reproduce the externals of Skopas' style?

13. Tegea sculptures: see above, p. 75, n. 5. Palagia 1979, 213 criticizes my reconstruction of the akroteria of the temple and dissociation from it of the Herakles head, Tegea 48, but forgets (1) that the two large female torsos, my nos. 1 and 3, are not mirror images of each other but near duplicates, and so must come from opposite ends of the temple (for whose akroteria, Dugas' griffin, her preferred choice, is far too small), and (2) that the Herakles is not merely unique in having a *menískos* hole (actually, it has three), but is also too big, fully carved at the back, and turned in the wrong direction; cf. here now Stupperich 1980, 282. *Pace* Chamoux 1979, 564 and 1981, 13, the lion-skin cap and ears by no means certify my "Telephos," fig. 17, as a Herakles. First, the truncated cap is not a proper attribute of Herakles, whose leonine headgear on both coins and statues always includes the front paws of the animal knotted across his chest; and second, the ears of the helmeted head cited in the foregoing note are similarly cauliflowered: Stewart 1977 pl. 16. In my view, Telephos evidently adopted both features to link him as strongly as possible with Herakles, his father, whom we are told that he "most closely resembled" (Pausanias X. 28. 8; cf. here, for what it is worth, Jordanis, *Getica* IX, 59: [Telephus] *paternam fortitudinem propriis virtutibus aequans, Herculis genium formae quoque similitudinem referebat.* Alexander, himself descended from Herakles (Plutarch, *Alexander* II. 1), was to do exactly the same only a generation after this head was carved, presumably for the same reasons: von Graeve 1970, 148–50 and pls. 48–49; cf. 53. 2. For a number of corrections and further comments on my account, see Stupperich 1980, 280–83. The new metope head, loan no. L76.AA.13 (ht. 10 cm., Dolianà marble) is published by Frel 1980, 91 fig. 8.

14. Meleager: Stewart 1977, 104–07, pls. 44, 48d, 52; see now Lattimore 1973, 157–66 (unavailable to me at the time of writing *Skopas of Paros*) for a judicious analysis of the motif, although I am much less happy about whether his new "replicas" truly belong; also, I think that the appearance of the de Bry head should now lay to rest attempts to place the statue in the last quarter of the century and so dissociate it from Skopas himself: so Fink 1969, 239–52; Lattimore 1973, 166; 1975, 21; 1979, 77; Vierneisel-Schlörb 1979, 286 and 344, adheres to a date in the 330's, with which I would concur; cf Vermeule

1981 no. 51 (ca. 340). Concerning the attempt by Palagia 1979, 213 to relate the Meleager to the Giustini Asklepios see the résumé in Vierneisel-Schlörb 1979, 216–24; all else apart, the stance is different. Another new replica: Vermeule 1981 no. 52 (but not no. 53, which is an Ares Ludovisi).

The testimony of figs. 22 and 24 seems to confirm the penetrating analysis of the copies by Becatti 1940, 64–66, and supports his contention that the Medici–Fogg group of heads is closest to the original.

15. Pothos: Stewart 1977, 107–10, 127 no. 4 (Pliny, *Natural History* XXXVI. 25), 144–46, pl. 45. A second-century date for this statue is argued most recently by von Steuben 1966; Mingazzini 1971, 69, 75; Zanker 1974, 77; Vierneisel-Schlörb 1979, 485 n. 48. In the wake of my own studies on "neoclassical" sculpture (Stewart 1979, ch. 2) and after the discovery of the de Bry head, I see no reason to depart from my earlier view that the type is fourth-century in origin and is indeed Skopaic. The Conservatori statue (Stewart 1977, 145 no. G1, pl. 45a, c: here figs. 21–22) was already recognized as the most trustworthy replica by Bulle 1941, 147–48. The fact that it is not only a rather sensitive piece of sculpture in its own right but also the sole example of all those preserved that is truly close to the de Bry head might disturb those who still believe in the two axioms of *Kopienkritik* articulated by Lippold 1917, 97, 99–100, (1) that a mediocre sculptor is liable to be more faithful to his original, and (2) that sheer weight of numbers should determine what, in a series of copies, is truly "authentic." Compare, too, the parallel case of the Medici Meleager, above.

16. Samothrace, the Temenos: Lehmann 1973; Lehmann 1982 passim. The publication in *Samothrace* vol. V of Lehmann's final conclusions about this monument, announced in a lecture at The J. Paul Getty Museum on March 1st, 1979, is eagerly awaited. My own arguments (in Stewart 1977, 110, 146 no. H1, pl. 45b) for the addition of a Phaethon to this group, a statue which is in any case attested only in the weaker manuscripts of Pliny, will require revision in the light of Lehmann's work, which reached me only just before *Skopas of Paros* went to press. If the Salamis torso is not a "Phaethon," its nearness in style to the Pothos still requires explanation: one thinks of either the Eros or the Himeros from Skopas' group at Megara (Stewart 1977, 130 no. 27: Pausanias I. 43. 6); but to propose an attribution would, in the light of this one cryptic reference, be totally gratuitous (Chamoux 1979, XV, doubts that Skopas had any part in the Temenos program). On the Samothracian group see now Simon 1980 b.

At this point it is perhaps à propos to note Lehmann 1978, 67–71, an interesting contribution to the question of Skopas' archaistic work (to which I paid too little attention in *Skopas of Paros*).

17. Skopas' following: Stewart 1977, 115–24, pls. 46–51. For his influence on ruler portraits see e.g. Türkoglu and Atalay 1975, 123–50 (Lysimachos), and cf. the coin portraits of Philetairos: Westermark 1961, V.8–R.1; Boehringer 1972, pl. 12.

18. Revivals: Stewart 1977, 122; now corrected by Stewart 1979, 48–50, pls. 10–11, 15. Skopas' inclusion in a Pergamene or Alexandrian "canon" of top-rank sculptors is suggested by the papyri, *Laterculi Alexandrini* col. 7, 3–5 and *POxy* X. 1241. 13–5 (Stewart 1977, 135 no. 48, 151 no. 48bis), as well as by his frequent appearance with Pheidias and Praxiteles in the literary sources of the Roman period (Stewart 134–35, nos. 41–47).

19. Two descendents of his, a second Skopas and a second Aristandros, actually worked for the Romans in the first century: Stewart 1977, 135 nos. 49–52, 152 n. 25 (bibliography); see, most recently, Marcadé 1969, 541 s.v. "Aristandros."

20. Skopas at Rome: by the first century A.D., originals by Skopas were to be found

in the temple of Brutus Callaecus (Ares and Aphrodite), the temple of Apollo Palatinus (Apollo from Rhamnous), the temple of Cn. Domitius Ahenobarbus in the Circus Flaminius (Marine Thiasos), and the Gardens of Servilius (Hestia, basket-bearer): cf. Stewart 1977, 127–32 nos. 57–58, 11, 20, 32; on the Hestia, note Despinis 1965, 131–32 (from Paros?). In addition, three works only doubtfully attributed to him were also in Rome: a Niobid group, a Janus, and an Eros: Stewart 1977, 133 nos. 37–39. For the copies of Skopas' works see Stewart 1977, 139–46: N.B. that the Herakles Lansdowne was found in Hadrian's villa at Tivoli, and that a copy of it formed part of the decorative ensemble of the Villa dei Papiri (cf. Pandermalis 1971, 179–80, 202 no. 25): at Malibu a cast of this latter piece is exhibited close to its original find-spot, at the museum end of the lake in the garden peristyle.

21. Roman accounts of Skopas: Stewart 1977, 126–35.

The Achilles Head and the Tegea Sculptures
1. Dolianà marble: Stewart 1977, 39; and the Malibu head, Frel 1980, 91; Chamoux 1981, 8–9.
2. Scale of west pediment heads: Stewart 1977, 7–8, 34–35. Even though the head is in any case documented back to the 1830's (fifty years before anything from Tegea saw the light of day), the exactness of the fit (see below) in itself should dispel any lingering doubts concerning the piece's authenticity, since until very recently the prevailing orthodoxy was that the Tegea fragments displayed no such uniformity of scale: cf. Stewart 1977, 7–8.

Measurements (for NM 180 see Stewart 1977, 23 no. 17, 34–35, pls. 14–15).

	Malibu	NM 180
(1) GENERAL		
Total height	29.8	32.6
Max. width	23.0	22.8
Max. depth	26.3	26.8
(2) HEAD: VERTICAL		
Total height	26.5	25.0 (top cut away)
Chin to helmet rim	c.18.0	—
Below chin to base of nose	07.1	06.9
Below chin to base of canthus	12.2	12.3
Below chin to base of bridge	14.3	14.4
Below chin to base of helmet rim	18.5	18.3
Base of nose to bridge	07.2	07.5
Bridge to helmet rim	04.1	03.9
Outer corner of mouth to canthus	07.1	07.1
(3) HEAD: HORIZONTAL		
Outermost locks of hair	23.2	21.8
Temples	14.2	14.0
Before tragus of ear	16.1	15.9
Outer corners of eyes	09.6	09.7
Cheekbones	c.12.0	c.11.5
(4) HEAD: DEPTH		
Nose to back of helmet	29.3	26.8
Earhole to underside of chin	14.1	14.0

3. Chamoux 1981, 10–11, argues that the tenon and dowel hole are modern, which is by no means impossible. Yet there is other evidence of recutting at Tegea: several of the fragments carry dowel- or clamp-holes that could be secondary, e.g., a battered male head (Stewart 1977, 18 no. 10, pl. 8c–d) and a thigh fragment (Stewart 1972, 100 no. 32, pl. 17), both, to judge by their scale, from the east pediment.

4. Finish of Tegea heads: Stewart 1977, 40–43.

5. Iconography of the hunt, and helmets: Stewart 1977, 6, 23.

6. Optical corrections: Stewart 1977, 17–18, 48, 56–57; emendations by Stupperich 1980, 281–82. Chamoux 1981, 4–5, suggests the opposite viewpoint (cf. fig. 24), not realizing that the "less careful" chiseling of the details on the left side is secondary and that this side is the more weathered.

7. Achilles' hair: *Iliad* XXIII. 138–51; cf. Friis Johansen 1967, figs. 35, 40, 90, with, e.g., Simon-Hirmer 1976, pls. 51, XXV-VI, 117, 146–47, XLII and 183. On Alexander and Achilles see below, section 7, with Schwarzenberg 1967, 68–70; Hölscher 1971, 25–35.

Looking at the Head

1. Style of the Tegea heads: Stewart 1977, 73–76.

2. On "glyptic" and "plastic" modeling see in general Carpenter 1960, ch. 9, with Stewart 1979, 78, pl. 23a-b.

3. "Perseus" (Athens NM 13 396) and Polykleitan School: Lullies-Hirmer 1960, pls. 218–20; Arnold 1969, 207–10, pl. 27c; Bol 1972, 18–24, pls. 6–9.

4. "Aberdeen" head (BM 1600): On its Praxitelean affiliations, see Wolters 1886, 54–55; E. Sellers, in Furtwängler 1895, 346–47; Klein 1898, 388–89; on the differences, Ashmole 1922, 244, fig. 8; Pfuhl 1928, 23–24; Cook 1977, 77, pl. 23. Ancient connoisseurs seem to have perceived a certain affinity between Skopas and Praxiteles, which this comparison may help to illuminate: cf. Stewart 1977, 2–3, 104, 108, 113–14.

5. Skopas and "Ionian" sculpture: Stewart 1977, 72–73; contra, Schlörb 1965, 30–31. For the Lycian sarcophagus (fig. 5) see Lullies-Hirmer 1960, pls. 193–97 and p. 86, and on the (somewhat hybrid) characteristics of East Greek style at this date see in general Lippold 1950, 206–10; Childs 1973, 105–16, e.g., esp. fig. 1.

6. *Physiognomonica*: for most readers, the most accessible text and translation of this work will be that by W. S. Hett, in the Loeb series: Aristotle, *Minor Works* (Cambridge and London 1936), pp. 83–140; see also R. Foerster, *Scriptores Physiognomonici* vol. 1 (Leipzig 1893), 1–91. Recent studies of ancient physiognomics: Schmidt 1941, 1064–74;

Evans 1969. Select passages to illustrate Greek awareness of surface textures: *Iliad* XIII. 278–86; *Odyssey* XIX. 232–33; Aristophanes, *Clouds 1009–23;* Prodikos, *Choice of Herakles*, in Xenophon, *Memorabilia of Sokrates* II. 1. 21–22.

7. Urgency: Francotte 1916, 1431–32 (cf. Burford 1969, 97–99, 106–07) persuasively argues that the Tegean contract is above all concerned with the rapid completion of each stage of the work while funds were still to hand (for estimates of costs and Tegea's ability to meet them see Stewart 1977, 161 n. 91, although if the city actually owned or controlled the Dolianà quarries, this would have cut expenditure considerably). The ever-present threat of enemy action no doubt also played a part. In any case, and however motivated, the need to finish rapidly and the attendant penalty clauses eventually incorporated into the contracts seem to provide a better explanation for the negligence often noted in fourth-century architectural sculpture than the one that is more regularly advanced, namely, declining standards, however seductive this may be to present-day Western sensibilities.

8. Workshop "hands" at Tegea, and contrast with Praxiteles: Stewart 1977, 2–3, 67, 104, 113–14; Himerios, *Oratio* LXIV. 4 (ed. Colonna) = Overbeck 1868, no. 1300.

The Center of the West Pediment

1. Iconography of the west pediment: Pausanias VIII. 45.7; Stewart 1977, 22–30, 63–66, 133 no. 36 (Pausanias); on the theme, see Robert 1921, III. 1138–60; Bauchhenss-Thüriedl 1971; Delivorrias 1973, 111–35; Chamoux 1981, 12–15.

The earliest ancient accounts of the battle, written in the seventh century, were to be found in Hesiod's *Eoiai* (fr. 165 Merkelbach-West, = P. Oxy. 1359 fr. 1) and in the *Kypria* (Proclus, *Chrestomathia* I, p. 104, ed. Allen). The following later sources, arranged chronologically, describe it at some length:

(1) Euripides, *Telephos* (Page 1950, 10 no. 17; Handley-Rea 1957; Webster 1967, 44–45; with Accius frs. 14, 15 (Ribbeck) (5th B.C.)

(2) Lycophron, *Alexandra* 205–15 (3rd/2nd B.C.)

(3) Apollodorus, *Bibliotheca*, epit. III. 17 (1st A.D.)

(4) Philostratos, *Heroicus* II. 14–18, pp. 155–60, ed. Kayser (2nd/3rd A.D.)

(5) Dictys Cretensis, *Bellum Trojanum* II. 1–7 (2nd/4th A.D.)

(6) Dares Phrygius, *De excidio Troiae historia* 16 (5th A.D.—fantasy)

(7) Jordanis, *Getica* IX. 59–60 (6th A.D.)

(8) Tzetzes, *Antehomerica* 268–85 (12th A.D.).

Also the following scholia:

(9) Schol. B *ad Iliadem* I. 59; (10) Eustathius and *Iliadem* I. 59; (11) Schol. *ad Lycophronem* 206, 211.

The following sources give brief accounts and/or important information about the battle:

(a) Pindar, *Isthmian Odes*, V. 41, VIII. 48; *Olympian Ode* IX. 70 (5th B.C.)

(b) Delphic inscription to Dionysos Sphaleotas, Daux-Bousquet 1942–43, 119; 1942–43b, 20–24 (3rd/2nd B.C.)

(c) Seneca, *Troades* 213 (1st A.D.)

(d) Pausanias I. 4.6, VIII. 45.7, IX. 5.14 (2nd A.D.)

(e) *Anthologia Palatina* XVI. 110 (Philostratos, 3rd A.D.)—cf. IX. 477

(f) Hyginus, *Fabulae* 101 (2nd/4th A.D., perhaps plot of Euripides' *Telephos)*

(g) Quintus Smyrnaeus, *Posthomerica* IV. 41–42, 173–77; VII. 379–80; XIV. 130 (4th A.D.)

(h) Tzetzes, *ad Lycophronem* 1249; *Chiliades* XII. 951 (12th A.D.).

2. Hiera: Philostratos, *Heroicus* II. 18, p. 160 (ed. Kayser); cf. Tzetzes, *ad Lycophronem* 1249; *Antehomerica* 279; *Chiliades* XII. 951; Stewart 1977, 157 n. 154. Unfortunately the prologue of Euripides' *Telephos* breaks off at the crucial point: Handley-Rea 1957, 18–19. On the Telephos frieze of the Great Altar, whose iconography (following the discovery of the de Bry head) can now be seen to differ radically from Tegea, see Stewart 1977, 54, pl. 29c, with Robert 1887, 253; 1888, 99; Schrader 1900, 127, pl. 1; Winnefeld 1910, 56 and plan 2, scene 23. Considering the chronology of the battle set out by Philostratos, I cannot see why these studies often place Hiera's death *before* the wounding of Telephos, and I find it even more difficult to accept Bauchhenss' interpolation of what may be her prothesis (scene 10) into the middle of the battle.

3. Ankaios and east pediment: Stewart 1977, 50–53, 133 no. 36 (Pausanias VIII. 45. 6–7), pls. 9–11, 53; *contra*—but why, considering the evidence?—Stupperich 1980, 282.

4. NM 180: Stewart 1977, 23–24 (no. 17), 55, pls. 14–15, 53. Amongst the fragments, the defeated part of the Greek army is represented by at least one preserved head (Stewart 1977, 24 no. 18, pl. 16) and perhaps two (ibid. 27–28 no. 23, pl. 18).

5. Facial expression: Stewart 1977, 73–76.

6. Athena: Frel 1979, 6. A rather similar situation, but this time with Zeus's thunderbolt as the source of distraction, has recently been proposed for the west pediment of the Parthenon (a temple whose program Skopas seems to have wanted to echo at Tegea, at least to some extent: Stewart 1977, 66–67) by Simon 1980. Professor Evelyn Harrison informs me that a red-figured vase with such a scene was excavated at Pella in 1980.

7. Telephos and his "rightful victory"; Stewart 1979, 53–55 (although it is now clear that he cannot have been standing, as suggested there), 64. Apollodorus, Epitome III. 17, and Schol. B ad *Iliadem* I. 59, however, suggest a variant tradition in which it was Telephos who was running away. This, if not pure inference on the part of these writers themselves, cannot have found much sympathy at Tegea, where Telephos was *the* local hero. At Pergamon, where similar sentiments also prevailed, it is the Greeks who are routed: Winnefeld 1910, pls. 35, 5 and 36–38; Beil. 7, scenes 32–33.

8. Athena and Dionysos in the pediment: Picard 1954, 180–90; Delivorrias 1973, 115–19; Stupperich 1980, 281; cf. Stewart 1977, 63–65.

9. *Peripéteia*: Aristotle, *Poetics* VI. 17, 1450a34; XI. 1, 1452a22; cf. Lucas 1968, 127–34, Appendix 3; Burnett 1971, 1–10. Note in this context Euripides; *Andromache* 982; *Hercuba* 498; *Orestes* 367; and fr. 460 Nauck[2].

10. Tegean reverses, 362–338: Stewart 1977, 68–69, with list of sources in Hiller von Gaertringen 1913, pp. xx-xxi; cf. ibid. 1934, 113–14. Select passages: Diodorus Siculus XVI. 39; Pausanias IV. 28. 1–2; VIII. 27. 9–10; Polybius XVIII. 14.

11. Comparison with Mausoleum frieze: on BM 1007-8-10 see Ashmole 1969, 22–23, pl. 1; Ashmole 1972, 174–77, pls. 201–03; Stewart 1977, 97, pls. 40–41c. For doubts on the attribution see Cook 1979, 128–29 and Carter 1981, 189; their provisional conclusion, that as an architectural molding the frieze would have been supervised not by Skopas and his companions but by the architect, Pytheos (a position supported by the strong similarities recognized by Carter between slabs BM 1020–1 from the Mausoleum and the coffer reliefs from Pytheos' slightly later temple of Athena at Priene), deserves serious consideration. Cf. also Hornblower 1982, 225–31. The west pediment at Tegea involved figures 1.90 meters high set at 13 meters above ground level (Dugas 1924, pls. 12–14; Stewart 1977, 7–8, 22), while the Amazon frieze of the Mausoleum was only 90

centimeters high and set at around 20 meters above ground level (Waywell 1978, 55–56, fig. 8). Seen from the ground, then, the figures of the frieze would have seemed only about a quarter the size of their Tegean counterparts, a scale hardly conducive to complex narrative and difficult plots.

The Wrath of Achilles

1. *Areté* as a heroic ideal: Adkins 1960, chs. 1–4; less tendentiously, Fränkel 1975, 532–33 (with references). In the fourth century: Dover 1974, 67, 164–67, 235.
2. Priam from Epidauros: Schlörb 1965, 10, pl. 2; Stewart 1977, 74–75, pl. 26d. The date of this temple is still disputed, although all agree that it must precede Tegea (evidence in brief, Stewart 1977, 88) and must belong to the period ca. 400–370. Vierneisel-Schlörb 1976, 61–93 prefers a somewhat higher date (ca. 390) than I do, as does Stupperich 1980, 283.
3. Argive Heraion: for the heads see Waldstein 1902, pls. 30–33; a further head, now in the J. Paul Getty Museum, Frel 1979, 5 no. 13—although this (an Amazon) shows little of the extreme pathos of the male heads from the building. On *páthos* in general see Pollitt 1974, 184–89.
4. "Ares": Aeschylus, *Agamemnon* 78; Sophocles, *Electra* 1242; Euripides, *Phoenissae* 134.
5. "Lússa": cf. Aristophanes, *Plutus* 234.
6. Post-antique history of physiognomics; Lavater 1789–98; Goethe 1833; Baltrusaitis 1957, ch. 1 (with useful bibliography).
7. Leonine type: Note also in respect to the de Bry head the leonine connotations of the extended upper lip at *Physiognomonica* 6. 811a18; of a nose which is flat along the ridge and rounded at the tip (in profile view) at 6. 811b27; and of clouded brows at 6. 811b35 and 812a1. Cf. too the connection between flaring nostrils (as here) and a passionate character at 6. 811b3.
8. Vases with lion-predellas: eg. Broneer 1956, 345–49, pls. 50–51 (Beazley 1956, 145 no. 19, 148 no. 9).
9. Origins of the Tegea style: cf. Stewart 1977, 73–76, 85–89.
10. *Phthónos*, Artemis and Dionysos: Stewart 1977, 61, 63–65.

Skopas and the Heroic Temper

1. Herakles in the fourth century: see esp. Galinsky 1972, 101–07. No independent art-historical study of the sculpture exists; the vases have been discussed by Metzger 1951, 191–230; on Herakles in general see Robert 1921, II. 422–648; Burkert 1977, 319–24; iconographical sketch, with bibliography: Sichtermann 1960, 378–87.
2. Herakles and *pónos*: Aristophanes, *Clouds* 1048–52; Antisthenes (pupil of Socrates), three treatises recorded in Diogenes Laertius VI. 2, 16, 18, plus a quotation in a Syriac papyrus of Themistios, *On Areté*, ed. Gildemeister-Bücheler 1872, 450—51 (tr. Galinsky 1972, 107); Isokrates V. 109–12. The crucial text, however, is Prodikos' *Choice of Herakles* of ca. 430, as reported in Xenophon. *Memorabilia of Sokrates* II. 1. 21–34.
3. Sikyon Herakles: see p. 75, n. 3 above.
4. Herakles of Polykleitos: Arias 1964, 25–27, pls. XVI, 49–55; Lorenz 1972, 30–31, pls. 12–13. The lowered right arm probably held the club, its business end resting on the ground.
5. Vases with apotheosis and apples: Thompson 1949, 253–55, esp. pl. 61, 2; Metzger 1951, 210–24.

6. Sikyonian cult of Herakles: Pausanias II. 10.1, cf. Herodotus II. 44. White poplar: Servius, *Commentary on Vergil's Eclogues* VII. 61, cf. Macrobius, *Saturnaliorum* III. 12. 1–3; Harpokration s.v. *"leuké,"* etc.

7. Lansdowne Herakles: see p. 75, n. 7 above. Vase: Stewart 1977, pl. 42d.

8. Doryphoros of Polykleitos: Arias 1964, 21–25, pls. VII-X, 30–47; Lorenz 1972, 4–17, pls. 1–3, 22–29; von Steuben 1973, 11–55, pls. 1–39; Robertson 1975, 328–31, pls. 109–10. The identification as Achilles, which is not certain, rests on the following grounds: (1) the statue, almost seven feet tall, is of heroic scale; (2) the *dóru* is not an athlete's but a hero's weapon; specifically, Achilles' *dóru* was the most massive of all (*Iliad* IX. 412–15); (3) Pliny, *Natural History* XXXIV. 18 tells us that nude youths holding spears, called "images of Achilles," were popular in Roman gymnasia: several copies of the Doryphoros have been found in such contexts (cf. here Quintilian V. 12. 21); (4) the bronze Doryphoros herm from the Villa dei Papiri was placed opposite another of an Amazon (cf. Pandermalis 1971, 184–85, 206 nos. 51–52, pl. 84, 1: replicas of these are displayed at Malibu at the western end of the lake in the garden): an identification as Achilles and Penthesilea seems indicated; (5) Augustus chose the type as the model for his portrait statue perhaps with its Achillean associations in mind: Ovid, *Tristia ex Ponto* I. 7. 49–53. Perhaps the most telling evidence, however, is Lysippos' imitation of the statue for his Alexander/Achilles with the lance: see below, p. 60; further bibliography and discussion: Schwarzenberg 1967, 106 n. 66.

9. Lansdowne Herakles and Doryphoros: (1) as regards the pose, an intermediary may have been a Herakles by Polykleitos' follower Antiphanes, made from an Argive dedication at Delphi in the 360's: Arnold 1969, 190, 193–94, 198–99, pl. 26b; (2) in its proportions the Lansdowne statue in fact differs only marginally from the Polykleitan norm:

DIMENSIONS (cm.)

	Total height	Head, height	Torso, height	Torso, width	Legs, length
Doryphoros:	199.2	28.4	62.4	39.5	102.4
Herakles:	196.4	27.4	58.7	38.5	101.8

PROPORTIONS

	Head height: total height	Torso height: total height	Torso width: total height	Torso height: legs	Legs: total height
Doryphoros:	1:7.014	1:3.192	1:1.579	1:1.641	1:1.945
Herakles:	1:7.168	1:3.345	1:1.524	1:1.734	1:1.929

Specifically, the head is now very slightly smaller, the torso a little more compact, and the legs rather longer. These proportions are closer to Polykleitos' than those of many of the statues ascribed to his own school. Yet Skopas' adjustments to the canon are just sufficient, it seems to me, to substitute for Polykleitan balance between the parts a slight attenuation of form that, aided by the rising diagonals of the relaxed leg and club, tends now to draw the spectator's attention upward to the powerful features of the face, which now becomes the focal point of the composition and the prime agent for the hero's projection of his personality onto his environment. (3) The physique shows a similar ambivalence toward the Polykleitan ideal. While the architecture of the torso is at first sight very reminiscent of Polykleitan practice (but see Schweitzer 1952, 108 on the copyist's possible contribution here), the treatment of the individual muscles is very different. To quote Arnold (1969, 230 n. 780):

> The body is not built up from an organic arrangement of separate parts, each in definite relationship to the next, but comprehended as a single, heavy mass.

In fact, one could hardly find a better example of what a work looks like that is at once deeply indebted to Polykleitos and his followers but absolutely refuses to incorporate what is for them a normative principle, namely the hierarchical organization of parts. The Tegea fragments, it seems to me, support this assessment: cf. Stewart 1977, 71–72.

10. "What man is worth": Antisthenes, in Gildemeister-Bücheler 1872, 450–51.

11. Eclectic Herakles types: Arnold 1969, 197; Stewart 1977, 116, 173 n. 15.

12. Meleager: see p. 76, n. 14 above. For the story and sources see Robert 1921, II. 88–100; Stewart 1977, 60 (though one text, Bacchylides V. 56–175, was inadvertently omitted from my list at p. 159 n. 16).

Beyond Skopas

1. Lysippos: for accounts of his career, with bibliographies, see Johnson 1927; Giuliano-Ferri 1961; Sjöqvist 1964; Robertson 1975, 463–70, pls. 147–48. The ancient sources are collected by Overbeck 1868, nos. 1443–1512 (selection, translated, Pollitt 1965, 143–51), and more recently (with many more entries) by Moreno 1974. On his artistic principles see, in general, Sjöqvist 1966; Moreno 1973; Stewart 1978.

2. Weary Herakles: latest study, Vermeule 1975.

3. Sikyonian coins: Newell 1959, 17 no. 27, pls. 8, 18; Sjöqvist 1966, figs. 17–19; Vermeule 1975, 324 (with discussion of evidence for alternative location in Athens). Cf. Pausanias II. 9.8, and for an extended, though partially erroneous description of it (though with no word on its location or authority), Nikolaos of Myra, *Progymnasmata* 15 (in Libanius, ed. R. Foerster, vol. VIII. p. 500); translation, Pollitt 1965, 148–49.

4. Erotes at Thespiae: Pausanias IX. 27.3.

5. Lysippos and Alexander; Pliny, *Natural History* VII. 125; Plutarch *On the Fortune of Alexander* II. 2, 335A; *Alexander* IV. 1; etc. On Lysippos and Alexander see esp. Schwarzenberg 1967; Hölscher 1971; Schwarzenberg 1975; Yalouris et al. 1980, 98–99 no. 2.

6. Alexander and Achilles: Plutarch, *Alexander*, V. 5, XV. 4–5, etc.; cf. Schwarzenberg 1967, 68–70. In my view, the "Rondanini" statue in Munich shows Alexander as Achilles arming, after *Iliad* XIX. 364–91, esp. 369–70: cf. Hölscher 1971, 25–30; Schwarzenberg 1975b; Vierneisel-Schlörb 1979, 370–79, figs. 180–88. Since the appearance of the Alsdorf relief (Vermeule 1971, 176, pl. 45; Koch 1978, 116–35; Yalouris et al. 1980, 119, no. 40), the already fearsome problems surrounding this statue have become immeasurably more complicated, and now is not the place to engage them. On Lysippos' statues of Alexander see the previous note; they were of "heroic" size, just as the Polykleitan Achilles was: Choricius XXXVII (*Dial.* 23), *Cod. Madr.* fol. 174[V] = Förster 1894, 168.

7. Theories of vision: Empedokles 31 B 84 (Diels-Kranz[7]); Demokritos 68 A 135, section 50 (Diels-Kranz[7]); Plato, *Timaeus* 45C; *Theaetetus* 156 D-F; Aristotle, *De Anima* III. 12, 345a:10; *De Sensu* II. 437a 23-439a 6 (with quotation from Empedokles); *De Partibus Animalium* II. 1, 657a25-33; Theophrastos, *De Sensu* X. 50 (with précis of Demokritos); cf. Schwarzenberg 1967, 70–72; Clark 1975, 68–83; Lloyd 1975, 218–22.

8. Lysippos misunderstood as a realist by both ancients and moderns; Schwarzenberg

1975, 253; Stewart 1978, 168. One should note in this context (1) that his aim was not "truth to nature" itself, but the *illusion* of truth (Pliny, *Natural History* XXXIV. 65) and (2) that when Quintilian criticizes Demetrios of Alopeke for his realism, he praises Praxiteles and Lysippos together for having the "best"—i.e., *most satisfactory*—approach to nature (Quintilian XII. 10.9). He sought, in fact, to convince the observer of the truthfulness of his work while subtly idealizing his sitter's features, aiming at a *more* than natural grace and the appearance of greater height (Pliny, *Natural History* XXXIV. 6, 5–6); cf. here Pollitt 1975, 321, 362–65, 378–79.

9. Ares Ludovisi: Stewart 1977, 116–17, pl. 48; Lattimore 1979; Vierneisel-Schlörb 1979, 424–29; Raftopoulou 1980, 388–93. The new head, whose face must have lain in water to judge by the pronounced tidemark running from the crown to the ears and the base of the neck, is of Pentelic marble and measures 39.2 centimeters in height. Another new replica: Vermeule 1981 no. 53 (misidentified as a Meleager).

10. Herculaneum fresco and group in Rome: Pliny, *Natural History* XXXVI. 29; Sichtermann 1957; Hölscher 1971, 49, pl. 9, 2.

11. Getty Alexander, 73.AA.27: Frel 1979, 7 no. 20; Yalouris et al. 1980, pl. 2, p. 101 no. 6. The artist seems to have been the Athenian who made the "Ariadne" from the south slope of the Akropolis and who was perhaps responsible for the originals of the Uffizi Niobids: cf. Stewart 1977, 118–20, pl. 50.

12. Cults of Alexander: Habicht 1970, 17–36, 245–52. The question of whether he was worshiped in his lifetime seems at present to have little bearing on the monuments as we have them: see Hamilton 1973, 138–41 for a sensible statement of the evidence. It should be unnecessary to stress that Alexander did not get whatever ideas he had on self-deification from Persia: the Achaemenid monarchs were never worshiped as gods, in their lifetimes or after.

13. "Pothos" of Alexander: Ehrenberg 1938, ch. 2; comments by Hamilton 1973, 47, 175 n. 5. Alexander's grief for Hephaistion: Hamilton 1973, 145–46.

14. Skopas and ruler-portraits: see p. 77, n. 17 above.

Retrospect
1. Temple and altar: Pausanias VIII. 47.3; Stewart 1977, 50, 65, 68, 150.

Bibliography

Adkins, A.W.H. 1960. *Merit and Responsibility: A Study in Greek Values.* Oxford.

Arias, P.E. 1964. *Policleto.* Milan.

Arnold, D. 1969. *Die Polykletnachfolge. JDI* Ergänzungsheft 25. Berlin.

Ashmole, B. 1922. "Notes on the Sculptures of the Palazzo dei Conservatori." *JHS* 42: 238–47.

———. 1969. "A New Join in the Amazon Frieze of the Mausoleum." *JHS* 89:22–23.

———. 1972. *Architect and Sculptor in Classical Greece.* London.

Baltrusaitis, J. 1957. *Aberrations: quatre essais sur la légende des formes.* Paris.

Bauchhenss-Thüriedl, C. 1971. *Der Mythos von Telephos in der antiken Bildkunst.* Würzburg.

Beazley, J.D. 1956. *Attic Black-Figure Vase-Painters.* Oxford.

Becatti, G. 1940. "Attikà, saggio sulla scultura attica dell'ellenismo." *RIA* 7: 7–116.

Bingöl, O. 1980. "Die Figuraltrommeln des Apollon - Smintheus - Tempels (Vorbericht)." *Belleten* 44: 257–64.

Boehringer, C. 1972. *Zur Chronologie mittelhellenisticher Munzserien, 220–160 v. Chr.* Berlin.

Bol, P.C. 1972. *Die Skulpturen des Schiffsfundes von Antikythera. AM* Beiheft 4. Berlin.

Broneer, O. 1956. "The North Slope Krater: New Fragments." *Hesperia* 25: 345–349.

Bulle, H. 1941. "Zum Pothos des Skopas." *JdI* 56: 121–150.

Burford, A. 1969. *The Greek Temple Builders at Epidauros.* Liverpool.

Burkert, W. 1977. *Griechische Religion.* Mainz.

Burnett, A.P. 1971. *Catastrophe Survived: Euripides' Plays of Mixed Reversal.* Oxford.

Carpenter, R. 1960. *Greek Sculpture.* Chicago.

Carter, J.C. 1981. "The Mausoleum, the Temple of Athena at Priene and Pytheos." *AJA* 85: 189.

Chamoux, F. 1979. "Du nouveau sur Scopas." *REG* 92: xv-xvii.

———. 1979b. Review of Stewart, *Skopas of Paros. REG* 92: 564—565.

———. 1981. "Un Chef-d'oeuvre de Skopas: la tête Michel de Bry," *Mon. Piot* 64: 1–16.

Childs, W.A.P. 1973. "Prolegomena to a Lycian Chronology." *OpRom* 9: 105–116.

Clark, S.R.L. 1975. *Aristotle's Man. Speculations upon Aristotelian Anthropology.* Oxford.

Cook, B.F. 1976. "The Mausoleum Frieze. *Membra Disjectanda.*" *BSA* 71:49–54.

———. 1979. "Neue Entdeckungen am Mausoleum von Halikarnassos." *AntK* 22: 128–9.

Cook, R.M. 1977. "The Aberdeen Head and the Hermes of Olympia." *Festschrift für Frank Brommer,* edited by U. Höckmann and A. Krug, p. 77. Mainz.

Daux, G., Bousquet, J. 1942-43. "Agamemnon, Télèphe, Dionysos Sphaléotas et les Attalides." *RA* 20: 113–125.

———, 1942-43b. "Agamemnon, Télèphe, Dionysos Sphaléotas et les Attalides." *RA* 20: 19–20.

Delivorrias, A. 1973. "Skopadikà (I)." *BCH* 97: 111–135.

Despinis, G.I. 1965. "Timitikon psifisma ek Parou." *ADelt* 97:119–32.

Diels, H., Kranz, W. 1954. *Die Fragmente der Vorsokratiker. Siebente Auflage.* Berlin.

Dover, K.J. 1974. *Greek Popular Morality in the Time of Plato and Aristotle.* Berkeley and Los Angeles.

Dugas, C., Berchmans, J., Clemmensen, M. 1924. *Le Sanctuaire d'Aléa Athéna à Tégée.* Paris.

Ehrenberg, V. 1938. *Alexander and the Greeks.* Oxford.

Evans, C.E. 1969. "Physiognomics in the Ancient World." *Transactions of the American Philosophical Society,* 59 no. 5.

Fink, J. 1969. "Der Grosse Jäger." *RM* 76: 239–252.

Förster, R. 1894. "Der Praxiteles des Choricius." *JdI* 9:167–190.

Francotte, H. 1916. "Industrie und Handel." Pauly-Wissowa, *Real-Encyclopedie der classischen Altertumswissenschaft* 9.2: 181–1439.

Fränkel, H. 1975. *Early Greek Poetry and philosophy.* tr. Moses Hadas. Oxford.

Frel, J. 1975. *Antiques in the J. Paul Getty Museum. A Checklist. Sculpture I: Greek Originals.* Los Angeles.

————, 1980. "The De Bry Head: Achilles by Scopas." *The J. Paul Getty Museum Journal* 8: 90–93.

Friis Johansen, K. 1967. *The Iliad in Early Greek Art.* Copenhagen.

Furtwängler, A. 1895. *Masterpieces of Greek Sculpture.* Edited by E. Sellers. London.

Galinsky, G. Karl. 1972. *The Herakles Theme.* Oxford.

Gildemeister, J., Bucheler, F. 1872. "Themistios Perì aretès." *RhM* 27: 438–462.

Giuliano, A., Ferri, S. 1961. "Lisippo." *Enciclopedia dell'Arte Antica,* vol. 4: 654–660. Rome.

Goethe, J.W. von. 1833. *Briefe von Goethe an Lavater aus den Jahren 1774 bis 1783.* Ed. H. Hirzel. Leipzig.

Graeve, V. von.. 1970. *Das Alexandersarkophag und seiner Werkstatt. Istanbuler Forschungen 28.*

Habicht, C. 1970. *Gottmenschentum und Griechische Städte. Zetemata* Heft 14. Munich.

Hamilton, J.R. 1973. *Alexander the Great.* London.

Handley, E., Rea, J. 1957. *The "Telephos" of Euripides. BICS* Supplement 5. London.

Hanfmann, G.M.A., Pedley, J. 1964. "The Statue of Meleager," *Antike Plastik* 3: 61–66. Berlin.

Hiller von Gaertringen, F. 1913. *Inscriptiones Graecae* v. 2. *Inscriptiones Arcadiae.* Berlin.

————. 1934. "Tegea." Pauly-Wissowa, *Real-Encyclopedie der classischen Altertumswissenschaft* 5A.1: 107–118.

Hölscher, T. 1971. "Ideal und Wirklichkeit in den Bildnissen Alexanders des Grossen." *Abh der Heidelberger Akademie, Phil.-Hist. Klasse,* no vol. number, no. 2.

Hornblower, S. 1982. *Mausolus.* Oxford.

Howard, S. 1978. *The Lansdowne Herakles.* Los Angeles.

Johnson, F.P. 1927. *Lysippos.* Durham.

Klein, W. 1898. *Praxiteles.* Leipzig.

Koch, G. 1978. "Zu einem Relief in der Alsdorf Foundation." *AA* 1978: 116–135.

Lattimore, S. 1973. "Meleager: New Replicas, Old Problems." *OpRom* 9: 157–166.

————. 1975. "Two Statues of Herakles." *The J. Paul Getty Museum Journal* 2: 17–26.

————. 1976. *The Marine Thiasos in Greek Sculpture.* Los Angeles.

————. 1978. Review of Stewart, *Skopas of Paros. AJA* 82: 415–416.

————. 1979. "Ares and the Heads of Heroes." *AJA* 83: 71–78.

Lavater, J.C. 1789-98. *Physiognomische Fragmente,* Eng. tr. as *Essays on Physiognomy,* ed. T. Holloway. London.

Lehmann, P.W. 1973. *Skopas in Samothrace.* Northampton.

————. 1978. "New Light on Skopas." *Bulletin of the American Society of Papyrologists* 15: 67–71.

————. 1982. *Samothrace* vol. 5: *The Temenos.* Princeton.

Linfert, A. 1966. *Von Polyklet zu Lysipp.* Dissertation, Freiburg University.

Lippold, G. 1917. "Zur Arbeitsweise römischer Kopisten." *RM* 32: 95–117.

————. 1950. *Die griechische Plastik. Handbuch der Archäologie* iii.. 1. Munich.

Lloyd, G.E.R. 1975. "The Empirical Basis of the Physiology of the Parva Naturalia." *Aristotle on Mind and the Senses. Proceedings of the Seventh Symposium Aristotelicum:* 215–239. Edited by G.E.R. Lloyd and G.E.L. Owen. Cambridge (U.K.)

Lorenz, T. 1972. *Polyklet.* Wiesbaden.

Lucas, D.W. 1968. *Aristotle's Poetics.* Oxford.

Lullies, R., Hirmer, M. 1960. *Greek Sculpture* (2nd edition). Munich.

Marcadé, J. 1969. *Au Musée de Délos.* Paris.

Metzger, H. 1951. *Les représentations dans la céramique attique du IVe siècle.* Paris.

Mingazzini, R. 1971. "Sui quattro scultori di nome Scopas." *RIA* N.S. 18: 69—90.

Moreno, P. 1973. *Testimonianze per la teoria artistica di Lisippo.* Treviso.

————. 1974. *Lisippo* I. Rome.

Newell, E.T., Noe, S. P. 1950. *The Alexander Coinage of Sikyon. Numismatic Studies no. 6.* American Numismatic Society, New York.

Norman, N. 1980. "The Temple of Athena Alea at Tegea: A Proposed Reconstruction of the Cella." *AJA* 84: 225.

Overbeck, J. 1868. *Die antiken Schriftquellen.* Leipzig.

Page, D.L. 1950. *Select Papyri* iii: *Literary Papyri: Poetry.* Cambridge and London (Loeb Classical Library).

Palagia, O. 1979. Review of Stewart, *Skopas of Paros. JHS* 99: 212–213.

————. 1980. *Euphranor.* Leiden.

Pandermalis, D. 1971. "Zum Programm der Statuenausstattung in der Villa dei Papiri." *AM* 86: 173–209.

Pfuhl, E. 1928. "Bemerkungen zur Kunst des vierten Jahrhunderts." *JdI* 43: 1–53.

Picard, C. 1954. *Manuel d'Archéologie Grècque* iv.1: *La Sculpture.* Paris.

Pollitt, J.J. 1965. *The Art of Greece, 1400–31 B.C. Sources and Documents.* Englewood Cliffs.

————. 1974. *The Ancient View of Greet Art.* Yale.

Raftopoulou, E.G. 1980. "Syschetisi thravsmaton kefalis sto Ethniko Archeologiko Mouseio." *Stili. Tomos eis mnimin Nikolaou Kondoleontos.* Pp. 338–393. Athens.

Ridgway, B.S. 1980. Review of Stewart, *Skopas of Paros. The Classical Outlook* 57.5: 114–115.

Robert, C. 1887. "Beiträge zur Erklärung des Pergamenische Telephos-Frieses I." *JdI* 2: 244–259.

————. 1888. "Beiträge zur Erklärung des Pergamenische Telephos-Frieses VI." *JdI* 3: 87–105.

————. 1921. *Die griechische Heldensage,* vols. ii-iii. Berlin.

Robertson, C.M. 1975. *A History of Greek Art.* 2 vols. Cambridge (U.K.)

Schlörb, B. 1965. *Timotheos. JdI* Ergänzungsheft 22. Berlin.

Schmidt, J. 1941. "Physiognomik." Pauly-Wissowa, *Real-Encyclopedie der classischen Altertumswissenschaft* 20.1: 1064–74.

Schrader, H. 1900. "Die Anordung und Deutung des Pergamenischen Telephos-Frieses." *JdI* 15: 97–135.

Schwarzenberg, E. 1967. "Der lysippische Alexander." *BJb* 167: 58–118.

————. 1975. "The Portraiture of Alexander." *Alexandre le Grand: image et réalité. Fondation Hardt, Entretiens* 22: 223–267. Geneva.

————. 1975b. "Zum Alexander Rondanini oder Winckelmann und Alexander." *Wandlungen. Studien...E. Homann Wedeking gewidmet.* Pp. 163–188. Waldsassen-Bayern.

Schweitzer, B. 1952. "Herakleskopf der Ny Carlsberg Glyptotek: Kopienkritisches zu Skopas." *JOAI* 29:101–111.

Sichtermann, H. 1957. "Zur Achill und Chiron-Gruppe." *RM* 64: 98–110.

————. 1960. "Eracle." *Enciclopedia dell'arte antica,* vol. 3: 378–387. Rome.

Simon, E. 1980. "Die Mittelgruppe im Westgiebel des Parthenon." *Tainia. Roland Hampe zum 70. Geburtstag...dargebracht.* Edited by H.A. Cahn and E. Simon. Pp. 239–256. Mainz.

————. 1980b. "A new statuette replica of the Pothos of Skopas." *Bull. of the Allen Memorial Art Museum, Oberlin College* 37.2: 71-76.

Simon, E. Hirmer, M. 1976. *Die Griechischen Vasen.* Munich.

Sjöqvist, E. 1964. "Lysippos." *Encyclopedia of World Art,* vol. 9: 357–362. New York.

————. 1966. *Lysippus. Lectures in Memory of Louis Taft Semple* II. Cincinnati.

Smith, A.H. 1916. "Some Recently Acquired Reliefs in the British Museum." *JHS* 36: 65–86.

von Steuben, H. 1966. Account of the Pothos in W. Helbig, *Führer durch die*

88

öffentlichen Sammlungen klassischer Altertümer in Rom, vol. ii: no. 1644. Edited by H. Speier. Tübingen.

————. 1973. Der Kanon des Polyklet. Tubingen.

Stewart, A. F. 1972. Skopas: the Sculptures of the Temple of Alea Athena at Tegea and related Works. Ph.D. dissertation, Cambridge (U.K.)

————. 1977. Skopas of Paros. Park Ridge.

————. 1978. "Lysippan Studies I. The Only Creator of Beauty." AJA 82: 163–171.

————. 1979. Attikà: Studies in Athenian Sculpture of the Hellenistic Age. JHS Supplementary Paper no. 14. London.

Stupperich, R. 1980. Review of Stewart, Skopas of Paros. Gnomon 52: 280–285.

Thompson, H.A. 1949. "The Pedimental Sculpture of the Hephaisteion." Hesperia 18: 230–268.

Türkoglu, S., Atalay, E. 1975. "Ein frühhellenistischer Porträtkopf des Lysimachos aus Ephesos." JÖAI 50: Beiblatt, 123–150.

Vafopoulou-Richardson, C.E. 1979. Review of Stewart, Skopas of Paros. CI Rev 29: 117–118.

Vermeule, C.C. 1971. "Dated Monuments of Hellenistic and Graeco-Roman Popular Art in Asia Minor: Pontus through Mysia." Studies Presented to George M.A. Hanfmann. Mainz. 169–176.

————. 1975. "The Weary Herakles of Lysippos." AJA 79: 323–332.

————. 1981. Greek and Roman Sculpture in America. Malibu and Berkeley.

Vierneisel-Schlörb, B. 1976. "Nochmals zum Datum der Bauplastik des Asklepiostempels von Epidauros." Festschrift G. Kleiner, pp. 61–93. Tübingen.

————. 1979. Glyptothek München: Katalog der Skulpturen. Bd. II: Klassische Skulpturen. Munich.

Waldstein, C. 1902. The Argive Heraeum, vol. I. Boston and New York.

Waywell, G.B. 1978. The Free-Standing Sculptures of the Mausoleum at Halicarnassus in the British Museum. London.

Webster, T.B.L. 1957. The Tragedies of Euripides. London.

Winnefeld, H. 1910. Altertümer von Pergamon iii. 2: Die Friese des grossen Altäres. Berlin.

Wolters, P. 1886. "Mitteilungen aus dem British Museum." JdI 1: 54–64.

Yalouris, N., Andronikos, M., Rhomiopoulou, K., Herrmann, A., Vermeule, C.C. 1980. The Search for Alexander: an exhibition. New York.

Zanker, P. 1974. Klassizistische Statuen. Mainz.

Photograph Credits

The photographs were provided by the institution that owns the object unless otherwise specified.

Alinari	40, 61
B. Ashmole	13, 14
Author	3, 7, 8, 17, 20, 21, 22, 33, 34, 50, 58
Deutsches Archäologisches Institut, Athens	4, 32, 35, 39
Deutsches Archäologisches Institut, Rome	51, 54
J. Frel	23
Hirmer Fotoarchiv	5, 53, 59
D. Hull	6, 18, 49

Photography of Getty Museum works of art by Donald Hull and Penelope Potter.
Drawings (figs. 2, 12, 15, foldout) by Martha Breen Bredemeyer.
Designed by Patrick Dooley
Typography by Marchese Graphics, Incorporated
Printing by Gardner/Fulmer Lithograph